# THE ESSENTIAL VEGAN INDIAN COOKBOOK

# THE ESSENTIAL
# Vegan Indian
## COOKBOOK

## 100 Homestyle Classics and Restaurant Favorites

PRIYA LAKSHMINARAYAN

**Photography Hélène Dujardin**

ROCKRIDGE
PRESS

For general information on our other products and services or to obtain technical support, please contact our Customer Care Department within the United States at (866) 744-2665, or outside the United States at (510) 253-0500.

Rockridge Press publishes its books in a variety of electronic and print formats. Some content that appears in print may not be available in electronic books, and vice versa.

Interior and Cover Designer: Amanda Kirk
Art Producer: Hannah Dickerson
Editor: Anne Lowrey
Production Editor: Andrew Yackira
Production Manager: Holly Haydash

Photography © 2021 Hélène Dujardin, food styling by Anna Hampton
Decorative pattern used under license from Shutterstock.com
Author photo courtesy of Cassandra Boryszak, Rooted Love Photography

Paperback ISBN: 978-1-63807-201-0
eBook ISBN: 978-1-63807-176-1
R0

To my Amma, Shyamala, and my Appa,
Lakshminarayan, who taught me to persevere.
Thank you for giving me wings to fly.

# Contents

# Introduction

If someone had told seven-year-old me, as I stood by my mother in the kitchen watching her cook, that I would author a cookbook someday, I would have believed it!

In fact, looking back at my life now, it feels as though I was always working toward this very moment.

When I was a child, my mother's okra recipe was published in a leading newspaper. Everyone in my family was thrilled to see her name in print. My father even saved that newspaper clip. I remember her beaming face and how proud she was.

It was then the desire to see my name in print was born.

As a child, I loved watching cooking and craft shows. I would host my own pretend cooking shows at home when no one was around. Those are some of my fondest childhood memories.

When I entered college, I chose home science as my major. I finally got a formal understanding of the science behind food and nutrition. By then, I was cooking regularly for my family and friends, and it boosted my confidence when I saw how well my food was received. I began getting cookbooks as birthday gifts, and bringing dishes from those books to life was, and still is, one of my favorite pastimes. I secretly wished to be a cookbook writer.

But then life happened, and my dream got pushed to the back burner.

Fast-forward to 2016, post marriage and settling in the United States, when I started a website to document my mother's recipes and my culinary experiments. Soon, I realized that this is what I wanted to do. This is how my blog *Cookilicious* (name coined by my brother) was born. This is my sacred place where I share vegetarian and vegan recipes, among other things I like to do.

I feel that my culinary palate is heavily influenced by my parents. My mother hailed from Trichy, a town in South India, and then settled in Bombay. Her cooking reflected her experiences with different cultures. My father, also from Trichy, lived most of his life in the west of India—Bombay and briefly in Gujarat. Naturally, his food choices were a little different from my mother's. Growing up, my brother and I were treated to this wonderful mix. My father would prepare dishes such as tomato omelet or French toast, whereas my mother would stick mostly to traditional South Indian fare.

Growing up in a cosmopolitan place like Bombay also worked in my favor. I got to sample many kinds of Indian cuisine, courtesy of my neighbors and close friends, who hailed from different parts of India.

Cooking vegetarian food comes naturally to me because my family has been vegetarian for generations. India is home to many vegetarians, yet veganism is a relatively new concept that is just taking root there. In a country where dairy products are an integral part of the cuisine, going vegan can be a daunting prospect. However, when I started blogging, I realized that most Indian recipes are naturally vegan or can be made vegan with just a tweak or two.

Many people may feel overwhelmed by the breadth of Indian food and limit their knowledge to just a few dishes. Moreover, vegans may eschew Indian food altogether because they feel the cuisine lacks vegan options or is too much work to make.

This book is here to show you that cooking vegan Indian food is not only possible, but easier than you might expect. The recipes primarily present a vegan take on traditional Indian recipes.

Through this book, I hope to take you on a journey through India and show you that Indian cooking can be made vegan without compromising on taste or convenience. I hope you find this book useful and enjoy dipping into some wonderful vegan Indian dishes.

Happy cooking!

# CHAPTER 1

# The Vegan Indian Kitchen

S teeped in the wonderful aroma of spices, the Indian kitchen in my childhood home was a magical place where my parents would transform seemingly mundane ingredients into mouthwatering delicacies.

In this chapter, I will introduce you to basic pantry staples such as spices, herbs, and other ingredients that you will be using for the recipes in this book and that will transform your own kitchen into a fragrant haven. We will also talk about some items of kitchen equipment that will make cooking the dishes simpler.

Lastly, we will go over a few basic cooking techniques that will enable you to prepare Indian dishes easily.

# Indian Cooking, the Vegan Way

As mentioned, many Indian recipes are either naturally vegan or can be made vegan with a few easy substitutions. Meat and dairy products feature in many traditional Indian recipes. People may believe that simply omitting them will adversely affect the flavor of a dish. For many vegans wanting to cook Indian food, this problem effectively reduces the number of recipes they can try or maybe even causes them to give up on Indian food altogether. However, I would like to dispel this notion. By making a few thoughtful substitutions, we can create vegan versions of any dish without compromising on taste.

## Vegan Substitutes

Here is a list of the most common animal products in Indian cuisine and what you can use in their place.

### DAIRY SUBSTITUTES

Many Indian recipes rely heavily on dairy products, but does that mean we have to give up on those dishes? Fortunately, the answer is no. With a few simple substitutions, dairy-containing recipes can be made vegan.

**Ghee:** Ghee imparts a fatty richness and an amazing aroma. The most widely used substitute for ghee is oil; coconut oil or any kind of vegetable oil will do the trick. To get the richness that ghee offers, though, use vegan butter or any plant-based margarine. On page 142 you can find a recipe for vegan ghee that comes close to the real thing. You can use it whenever a savory recipe calls for ghee or oil.

**Paneer:** Paneer, or Indian cottage cheese, is used in a variety of dishes and desserts. It is a great source of protein and is made by curdling milk. A good substitute is tofu, which is made from soybeans and is similar in texture to paneer. Another option is soya chunks (a.k.a. textured vegetable protein, or TVP) or chickpea flour tofu. For any dessert that calls for paneer, silken tofu works well.

**Yogurt:** Yogurt is often added to marinades and sometimes to gravy. Plant-based yogurts make a good substitute. Vegan buttermilk can also be used to give a dish a mildly sour flavor. Cashew paste, poppy seeds, or cornstarch can be used to thicken gravies.

**Cream:** Vegan coffee creamers are a great substitute for regular cream. You can also use cashew or coconut cream or soft silken tofu. For desserts, melted vegan ice cream is a great option.

**Milk:** It depends on the recipe, but coconut milk can sometimes be used; however, it has a strong flavor, so it should be used with caution. More neutral-tasting plant-based milk options, such as soy, almond, cashew (great for thickening curries), or oat milk can be used.

**Condensed milk:** Condensed milk is used in many Indian desserts. Plant-based condensed milk, such as almond or coconut, can be used as a substitute, or coconut cream.

### EGG AND MEAT SUBSTITUTES

Here are some substitutions that you can use in recipes that call for eggs, fish, chicken, or meat.

**Eggs:** Eggs are used extensively in Indian baking as a binding and stabilizing agent. A good substitute for eggs is aquafaba, which is the starchy liquid in a can of chickpeas. Another good substitute is flax egg, which is simply flaxmeal mixed with water. If you are making a curry or biryani where egg is the main ingredient, you can replace the egg with any vegetable of your choice.

**Meat and fish:** For meat- and fish-based recipes, you can replace the protein with vegetables such as eggplant or mushrooms, or tofu or soya chunks, because their texture is similar to meat. Alternatively, use any vegetable of your choice.

## Flavor-Building Techniques

In this section, we will talk about a few common Indian cooking techniques that build layers of wonderful flavor. Being familiar with these techniques and knowing which pitfalls to watch out for will help you take your cooking to the next level.

### FRESH INGREDIENTS

To get the best flavor profile possible, I suggest sourcing freshly grown herbs for your dishes. Dried herbs will work fine, but fresh ones will do wonders. Also, use fresh vegetables and fruits as much as possible.

### TOASTING SPICES

To make masalas (spice powders), we often toast spices without oil. Doing so helps the spices release their natural oils and increases their shelf life. The technique here is to roast the spice in a small pan over low to medium heat and stop as soon as the spice darkens in color and/or releases a fragrance. It is then cooled, ground, and stored in airtight containers. The time each spice takes to toast is different. I recommend that you toast each spice individually to avoid burning it. Here's a bit of trivia: Back in the day, spices were not toasted; they were sun-dried for days and then ground by hand using a mortar and pestle.

### TADKA (TEMPERING)

Tadka is the technique of frying whole or ground spices in oil or ghee. This technique is used mostly at the beginning of the recipe but can sometimes also be used at the end. It adds flavor to the dish because the oil becomes infused with the essence of the spices. To temper spices, pour some vegetable oil into a pan and place over low to medium heat. Allow the oil to heat up a little. Add a single mustard seed to the oil. If the seed sinks, the oil is not hot enough. If it pops within a short period of time, the oil is ready for tempering. To avoid burning the spices, fry them for a very short amount of time, maybe 5 to 10 seconds, before adding the next ingredient in the recipe.

### BHUNAO (SAUTÉING)

This step usually comes after tadka. *Bhunao* loosely translates to sauté or stir-fry. In this step, ingredients such as chopped onions, tomatoes, garlic, ginger, cashew paste, or any freshly ground masalas are sautéed in oil over medium to high heat. To ensure that the ingredients do not burn or stick to the bottom of the pan, a small amount of water, stock, or even yogurt is added. The sautéing continues until the oil separates from the spice mixture, at which time the vegetables and other ingredients are added.

### DUM (STEAMING)

Dum is a cooking technique in which the food is slowly cooked in its own juices over low heat. The cooking vessel is usually sealed, and the food cooks with the help of the trapped steam. This technique is often used to make rice dishes such as biryani, dishes such as korma, and even dal.

## TALNA (DEEP-FRYING)

Snacks such as pakoras and fritters require this technique. To deep-fry, pour vegetable oil into a kadhai (an Indian-style wok) and heat it over low to medium heat. After a few minutes, drop a bead-size portion of batter into the oil. If the batter sinks, the oil is not yet hot enough. If the batter rises to the top immediately, the oil is too hot, so reduce the heat a little and then begin frying. If the batter slowly floats to the top, the oil is at the correct temperature. During the frying process, keep turning the food so that all sides get evenly fried. Have a plate lined with paper towels ready to hold the fried items. The paper towels will soak up any excess oil.

# Equipping Your Kitchen

In any profession, the right tools make the job a lot easier. Cooking is no exception to this rule. The mantra "work smart, not hard" applies to the cooking world as much as it does to our daily lives. Investing in good equipment will not only make your life in the kitchen easier but will make cooking a pleasure, too. Here is a list of kitchen gadgets and equipment that I find very handy.

## Measuring Spoons and Cups

You'll need a set of measuring spoons that can measure from 1 teaspoon up to 1 tablespoon, and a measuring cup set (US standard) that can measure ¼, ⅓, ½, ¾, and 1 cup.

## Spice Box (masala dabba)

This is usually a round container with 4 or 5 smaller containers inside to hold spices and masalas. I keep mine within arm's reach of my cooktop, so I have easy access to my favorite spices while I cook.

## Knife and Chopping Board

I cannot stress enough the importance of a good-quality knife set and cutting board. Nothing is more frustrating than a dull blade that makes chopping a chore and can even be dangerous. Invest in a set of good-quality stainless steel knives, a knife sharpener, and a wooden chopping board.

## Vegetable Chopper

Many recipes call for finely or coarsely chopped vegetables or even vegetable slices. A vegetable chopper is a handy tool for this very purpose. It makes chopping vegetables such as onions, potatoes, or tomatoes a breeze.

## Mortar and Pestle

I always use a mortar and pestle to crush ginger, chiles, and garlic because doing so really brings out the juices and adds to the flavor of the dish. You can always use a knife to chop them, but in my opinion, that does not release as much flavor.

## Mixer Grinder

I would recommend investing in a good Indian mixer grinder. This is one of the most useful gadgets I possess. It comes with multiple attachments, each with a different blade and purpose. You can use it to make chutneys, spice powders, batters, and even juices.

## Food Processor

I have a food processor with a grating attachment. It makes shredding and grating vegetables a cinch. It also has a snap-on dough blade that allows the processor to knead any kind of dough.

## Pressure Cooker

A pressure cooker, electric or otherwise, to steam or pressure cook vegetables, lentils, and even rice is very useful. I use both cooktop and electric pressure cookers. The electric cooker (Instant Pot) is my go-to for one-pot recipes. But when I am steaming things like bafauri, I use the cooktop pressure cooker.

## Storage Containers

To store leftover food or ingredients, invest in silicone storage containers rather than plastic ones. They can store both hot and cold foods, are a breeze to clean, and, most important, are eco-friendly.

## Cookware

I prefer good-quality, stainless steel kadhai/woks, pots, and pans. Choose cookware with thick bottoms so the food will not stick and burn.

## Tawa (griddle)

A tawa (or griddle) is traditionally round, though there are a few square ones out there. Made of cast iron, nonstick, or stainless steel, it is perfect for making flatbreads, pancakes and crepes.

# The Plant-Based Pantry

Apart from the dairy and meat substitutes listed earlier, I have compiled a list of ingredients that you will need. If you keep these ingredients in stock, you'll have everything you need to make the recipes in this book. The key to Indian cooking is knowing when and how to add these ingredients and in what proportion, sequence, and combination. Each ingredient has a role to play in bringing out the flavor of the dish.

## Spices and Herbs

Spices and herbs form the base of many Indian dishes. Adding the right ones to a dish augments the flavor profile.

### MUST-HAVE

**Asafetida (hing):** A very little of this pungent spice powder is added to the tadka. It aids digestion and helps prevent flatulence. It contains wheat, so it is not gluten-free.

**Black salt (kala namak):** Black salt has a mild egglike flavor with a strong sulfuric odor. It is mainly used in chaat (street food) recipes because of its smoky taste. Contrary to its name, it is pink in color.

**Cilantro (dhaniya):** Fresh cilantro is added as an aromatic garnish toward the end of the recipe.

**Curry leaves (kadi patta):** Curry leaves are added at the tempering stage to add a distinctive flavor to curries, gravies, chutneys, spice mixes, and stews.

**Dill (shepu):** This herb has a strong earthy flavor that works great when mixed in flatbread dough or cooked with legumes.

**Green chiles:** There are a variety of green chiles that can be differentiated based on their heat levels. The smallest are the spiciest. Jalapeños and serrano peppers are a great substitute for the Indian green chile. Adjust the number of chiles in a recipe depending upon their heat and your tolerance level.

**Mint (pudina):** This aromatic herb gives a refreshing boost to chutneys and drinks, as well as other dishes.

**Red chiles:** Dried red chiles are added for color and heat. You can add them whole during the tadka or grind them along with other ingredients.

**Saffron:** Saffron is used in savory and sweet dishes for color and for its distinctive yet subtle rich, aromatic flavor.

**Seeds:** Cumin (jeera), coriander (dhania), fenugreek (methi), sesame (til), mustard (rai), and fennel (saunf) are some of the most commonly used seeds in everyday Indian cooking. They are used whole or in powdered form, depending upon the recipe. They are added to the tadka or combined to make a specific spice mix.

**Whole spices:** Whole spices are an integral part of Indian cuisine. In addition to their flavor, they are known for their anti-inflammatory and antioxidant properties. They are used whole or sometimes as ground powder. If in ground form, they are roasted first to help release more flavor and to increase their shelf life. Bay leaves (tej patta), cloves (laung), cinnamon (dalchini), and cardamom (elaichi) are some of the basic spices and can be used in savory and sweet recipes.

### NICE TO HAVE

These ingredients add certain complex flavors to dishes. However, they can be substituted or skipped.

**Ajwain or carom seeds:** These help digestion and are often added to dishes containing complex carbs. The seed has a distinctive flavor and aroma and is used as a natural preservative in jams, pickles, and chutneys.

**Fenugreek (methi) leaves:** Slightly bitter, these fresh greens are highly nutritious. They can be added to paratha dough, pancake batters, and even curries and rice.

**Kalonji (nigella) seeds:** These tiny black seeds have a nutty and peppery taste. They are mainly added to pickles and curries.

**Kasuri methi:** This is the slightly crisp sun-dried form of fenugreek leaves. It is normally added toward the end of the recipe or in marinades. The way to add it is to crush it between your palms and drop it into the dish. It helps enhance the flavor.

**Poppy seeds:** These nutty flavored seeds are used as thickening agents and to enhance flavor.

**Rasam powder:** This South Indian spice mix is used to make broths.

## MASALAS

Indian cooking is incomplete without masalas. Each masala has a role to play and helps bring out the true flavors of the dish. You can refer to chapter 7, where you will find recipes for easily making them at home. They are cost effective and can be made in bulk. Plus, they can be made without artificial colors or additives. You can buy them at a grocery store if you want to sample them first.

**Amchur powder:** This is dried mango powder that provides acidic flavors.

**Chaat masala:** Chaat means *lick* in Hindi. This spice mix gets its name because of its tangy flavors. It is added to snacks that require a certain punch.

**Chili powder:** There are many varieties of chili powder, depending on the variety of dried red chiles used. Some give only a deep red color and not much heat, whereas others add a lot of heat along with the color.

**Chole masala:** This spice blend is used when making chana masala.

**Garam masala:** This is one of the most popular and bold spice blends. It's prepared by dry-roasting a variety of aromatic spices. It is normally prepared in bulk and stored for months. It is added toward the end of the recipe before the garnish.

**Ground coriander:** Made by roasting and grinding coriander seeds, this powder comes in handy for flavoring anything savory.

**Ground cumin:** Similar to coriander powder, cumin is an aromatic spice that can elevate the flavors in a dish.

**Sambhar powder:** Made with a variety of dry-roasted spices, this South Indian spice blend is mainly used to prepare sambhar. However, you can also add it to stir-fries, rice recipes, or lentil stews.

**Turmeric:** This ground spice is a natural and powerful antiseptic. It lends a beautiful vivid yellow color to the dish along with its medicinal properties.

## Grains

These are the most common whole grains used in Indian cooking.

**Millets:** Ragi, bajra, and jowar are extremely nutritious, naturally gluten-free, and taste great. They can be used to make flatbreads, pancakes, snacks, and baked goods.

**Rice:** One of the staple foods of Indian cooking, regular white rice is served with any gravy, stew, or dal. Long-grain basmati rice is used when making pulao, pilaf, biryani, fried rice, any kind of flavored rice, and even desserts.

## Flours

There are many varieties of flour used in Indian cooking.

**Besan or garbanzo flour:** Made from split brown chickpeas, besan is mainly used in batters, fritters, desserts, and steamed snacks.

**Maida:** This finely milled bleached white flour is used to make breads, baked goods, street food, and fried dishes.

**Millet flour:** Millet is packed with vitamins and minerals and the flour can be used to make gluten-free flatbreads, pancakes, crepes, and baked goods.

**Rice flour:** Rice flour is mainly used in dough, batters, steamed food, and desserts. It adds crispiness to the dish.

**Semolina, sooji, or rawa:** A durum wheat product made by grinding husked wheat, semolina is extensively used in sweet and savory recipes.

**Wheat flour:** Wheat flour is used to make roti or chapati (Indian flatbread).

## Legumes

The superfoods in Indian cuisine, legumes are found in three forms: whole, split with the skin on, or split with the skin removed. When cooking with legumes, it's always advised to soak them first. This increases their nutrient density and promotes healthy digestion.

*Dal* most often refers to lentils and dishes made with lentils. Lentils are extremely versatile. They can be added to curries, stir-fries, soups, salads, stews, chilis, snacks, appetizers, and even desserts. Although they all cook in a similar way, the size, shape, and starch composition will determine the outcome.

**Black-eyed peas:** These legumes have an earthy flavor and a creamy consistency, and they are very easy to cook with.

**Black gram split and skinned lentils (urad dal):** Used in tempering, these give a nice crunch and flavor.

**Black gram whole lentils:** These are used to make dal and fermented batter.

**Chickpeas:** Brown (kala chana) and white chickpeas are versatile ingredients that are rich in proteins and carbs. They can be used to make a variety of recipes.

**Green gram split and skinned lentils (moong dal):** These are easy to digest and often used in khichdi and soups.

**Kidney beans (rajma):** Red kidney beans are popular in the north of India for vegan chilis, curries, and salads.

**Mung beans or sprouts:** These superfoods are rich in antioxidants and nutrients. Sprouting enhances their flavor and nutrition and makes them easily digestible.

**Pigeon peas (tur dal):** These legumes cook faster than the others.

**Red/pink/orange lentils (masoor dal):** These have an earthy flavor, and the longer they cook, the more they disintegrate.

**Split peas (chana dal):** This legume tends to hold its shape even after cooking.

## Other Ingredients

The ingredients in this section are must-haves in an Indian pantry.

**Chutneys:** Check out chapter 7 for some easy-to-make sweet and spicy chutneys.

**Coconut:** Another key ingredient in Indian cuisine, coconut can be freshly grated, dried, or flaked.

**Coconut cream:** Coconut cream is a great vegan substitute for cream (malai) to provide extra richness.

**Coconut milk:** Make it at home or buy it canned. Just remember to shake the can well before putting it in your cart. If you don't hear the liquid splashing around, don't buy it because it means the cream has hardened.

**Garlic:** Known for its strong flavor, garlic is one of the most beloved ingredients in many cuisines. Whether crushed in a mortar and pestle or minced to a paste, garlic makes a world of difference to a dish.

**Ginger:** This root is known for its pungent aroma and spicy flavor. Add ginger if you want that extra zing. You can use homemade or store-bought ginger-garlic paste instead.

**Lemon juice:** This ingredient acts as a natural salt and is often added as a final touch to a dish after garnishing. Because lemon has healing properties, wedges are always served as a side.

**Nuts and dried fruits:** Almonds, cashews, pistachios, dates, and dried figs are added to sweet and savory dishes either as thickening agents, as a garnish, or for crunch.

**Onions:** Onions bring a certain sweetness and crunch to a dish. Red onions are more popularly used in Indian cuisine. They can be consumed raw in salads or chaat, or they can be added to any savory dish.

**Peanuts:** Peanuts are added whole or coarsely chopped to snack and curry recipes, mainly to provide the required crunch.

**Tamarind:** This tart fruit has a sticky pulp with a sweet, sour, and tangy flavor. It can be consumed fresh, dried, or in pulp form.

**Tomatoes:** In any form—whole, pulp, puree, canned, or ketchup—tomatoes are used extensively in Indian cooking. They lend a deep red color and a tangy flavor.

## SHOPPING FOR YOUR INDIAN PANTRY

If you are looking to stock up your pantry to help you cook Indian food, check out the Resource section on page 153. Try to buy grains, lentils, and legumes in bulk from your local Indian grocer or from a retailer such as Costco. Consider buying legumes in dried form as it is more cost effective. Also, the spices at your local supermarket are high-priced in comparison to those at an Indian market. Shopping at an Indian grocery store is more economically viable, plus you'll find everything you need for your recipes under one roof. Store everything in airtight glass jars and it will last longer.

# About the Recipes

Indian cuisine by itself does not represent a single type of cuisine. Rather, it is a collective that encompasses many different regional cuisines. This makes it very diverse and versatile.

In this book, I have attempted to incorporate recipes from all over India. I have included popular recipes that are restaurant favorites as well as street food, plus classic recipes that have been passed down for generations. Some of these dishes are ones that I grew up with and are close to my heart. Also included are some fusion recipes that attempt to blur international boundaries.

The focus of this book is on dishes that you can make every day. Included, however, are delicacies to be served on special festive occasions. You will find a range of appetizers, entrees, soups, drinks, and desserts that showcase the diversity of Indian vegan cuisine.

I have tried to keep the number of ingredients and the prep times to a reasonable amount. The goal is to give you delicious recipes that you can easily whip up for breakfast, lunch, or dinner. Any ingredient from the Nice to Have section (page 8) is optional in my recipes. Adding the ingredient will enhance the flavor of the dish, but it is not required.

For every recipe, I have attempted to provide accurate cook times, but please note that these times may vary based on the equipment you have in your home.

A variety of tips were included to help you make the most of the recipes. You will see these as Ingredient tips (information about special ingredients), Prep tips (ideas to help you prepare the recipes more easily), and Variation tips (ways to change up the recipes to use different ingredients or techniques).

I have made each of these recipes multiple times, tweaking the ingredients and cook times to make sure they are reproducible every time, successfully. Whether you are trying vegan Indian cuisine for the first time or are a seasoned Indian chef, I sincerely hope you enjoy making these recipes as much as I enjoyed crafting them for you. Keep cooking delicious!

**Chatpata Aloo Salad (Crunchy Potato Salad) page 19**

# Salads, Starters, and Snacks

# Kachumber/Koshimbir
# (Mixed Vegetable Salad)

**PREP TIME:** 15 minutes • **SERVES 4**

This is a very popular, crunchy vegetable salad. In Northern India it is known as kachumber and is made without yogurt. However, in western India, it is called koshimbir and includes yogurt. Whichever version you choose, this salad can be made ahead of time and stored in the refrigerator. Use fresh vegetables for best results.

1 cup grated cucumber

½ cup grated carrot

½ cup finely chopped bell pepper (any color)

½ cup finely chopped onion

1 green chile pepper, minced

¼ cup chopped fresh cilantro

2 teaspoons ground cumin

¾ teaspoon salt

7 ounces plain unsweetened almond milk yogurt

1. In a large bowl, combine the cucumber, carrot, bell pepper, and onion and mix to combine.

2. Add the chile, cilantro, cumin, and salt. Mix again, and if not serving immediately, cover and place in the refrigerator.

3. When ready to serve, whisk the yogurt in a bowl and pour it onto the salad. Stir everything together well.

VARIATION TIP: You can replace the green chile with a serrano or jalapeño pepper, use parsley in place of the cilantro, and add crushed peanuts.

PER SERVING: Calories: 56; Total fat: 1g; Saturated fat: 0g; Sodium: 488mg; Carbohydrates: 9g; Sugar: 7g; Fiber: 2g; Protein: 4g

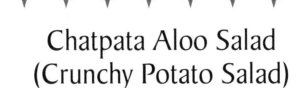

# Chatpata Aloo Salad
# (Crunchy Potato Salad)

**PREP TIME:** 20 minutes • **COOK TIME:** 5 minutes • **SERVES 4**

This crunchy salad hails from Nepal, which borders India in the northeast. The salad is prepared with a special masala called gorkha, and that, together with the tamarind, give the salad a unique flavor.

4 dried red chile peppers

2 tablespoons sesame seeds

2 teaspoons coriander seeds

2 potatoes, peeled, cooked, and cut into medium cubes

1 tomato, chopped

1 cup chopped cucumber

½ cup chopped onion

1 tablespoon tamarind paste or freshly squeezed lemon juice

¾ teaspoon salt

1 teaspoon vegetable oil

4 fenugreek seeds

2 green chile peppers, chopped

1. In a pan, dry-roast the red chiles, sesame seeds, and coriander seeds over medium heat for 5 minutes or until they become fragrant and change color.

2. Take the pan off the heat and allow the masala to cool completely.

3. Transfer the masala to a blender and coarsely grind. Set the masala aside.

4. Combine the potatoes, tomato, cucumber, and onion in a medium bowl.

5. Add the tamarind, masala, and salt. Mix everything together well.

6. Heat the oil in a tadka pan over low heat. Temper the fenugreek seeds and then fry the green chiles for 30 seconds.

7. Pour this tadka over the salad, give it a good mix, and serve.

PREP TIP: The potatoes should retain their shape when cut into cubes, so take care not to overcook them.

PER SERVING: Calories: 140; Total fat: 4g; Saturated fat: 0g; Sodium: 448mg; Carbohydrates: 24g; Sugar: 5g; Fiber: 4g; Protein: 4g

# Vaghareli Makai
# (Spiced Sweet Corn Salad)

**PREP TIME:** 5 minutes • **COOK TIME:** 20 minutes • **SERVES 4**

Mildly sweet and spicy, this corn salad hails from Gujurat. *Vaghareli* means "tempering" in Gujarati. This dish is a novel way to enjoy corn. For a delicious grilled flavor, you can husk the corn, grill it, and use the grilled kernels to make this salad.

1½ tablespoons coconut oil, divided

4 dried red chiles

1 tablespoon chana dal

1 tablespoon urad dal

1 tablespoon coriander seeds

1 teaspoon cumin seeds

14 curry leaves, divided

½ teaspoon chili powder

2 cups sweet corn kernels, thawed if frozen

2 tablespoons unsweetened shredded coconut

1 tablespoon vegan butter

1 teaspoon salt

1. Heat ½ tablespoon of coconut oil in a kadhai over medium heat. Temper the red chiles, chana dal, urad dal, coriander seeds, cumin seeds, and 7 curry leaves until the lentils turn golden, about 5 minutes. Transfer to a plate and let cool.

2. When cool, transfer the mixture to a mixer grinder and add the chili powder. Grind coarsely and set the masala aside.

3. To the same kadhai, heat the remaining 1 tablespoon of coconut oil and sauté the corn for 2 minutes.

4. Add the shredded coconut and the remaining 7 curry leaves and sauté for another 4 minutes.

5. Add the butter, ground masala, and salt. Cook for 30 seconds, then remove from the heat.

PER SERVING: Calories: 167; Total fat: 10g; Saturated fat: 7g; Sodium: 599mg; Carbohydrates: 21g; Sugar: 0g; Fiber: 3g; Protein: 3g

# Kosumalli Salad
# (Lentil and Pomegranate Salad)

**PREP TIME:** 10 minutes, plus 2 hours to soak • **COOK TIME:** 5 minutes • **SERVES 4**

This unique South Indian-style salad is made with soaked lentils, pomegranate seeds, and veggies. It's crunchy, colorful, and flavorful and is served at most traditional South Indian meals. Just soaking the dal makes it edible, so there's no need to cook it.

½ cup moong dal

¾ cup grated cucumber

⅓ cup grated carrot

¼ cup chopped fresh
cilantro

2 tablespoons freshly
squeezed lemon juice

⅓ cup
pomegranate seeds

¾ teaspoon salt

1 teaspoon vegetable oil

1 teaspoon
mustard seeds

6 curry leaves

¼ teaspoon
asafetida (hing)

1 green chile
pepper, minced

1. Rinse the moong dal and then soak in a bowl of water for 2 hours. Drain and transfer to another bowl.

2. Add the cucumber, carrot, cilantro, lemon juice, pomegranate seeds, and salt to the dal. Mix everything together well.

3. Heat the oil in a tadka pan. Temper the mustard seeds, curry leaves, asafetida, and green chile for 30 seconds.

4. Pour this tadka over the salad, mix, and serve.

**INGREDIENT TIP:** If you want to replace moong dal with another lentil, you'll need to cook the them al dente before using.

PER SERVING: Calories: 128; Total fat: 2g; Saturated fat: 0g; Sodium: 445mg;
Carbohydrates: 22g; Sugar: 4g; Fiber: 4g; Protein: 8g

# Soya-Stuffed Mirchi Pakora
# (TVP-Stuffed Fried Peppers)

**PREP TIME:** 30 minutes • **COOK TIME:** 15 minutes • **MAKES 8 PAKORAS**

Spicy mirchi pakora is a delicious fried appetizer. Here, the mirchi (pepper) is dipped in a thick batter and fried. Stuffing the pepper with textured vegetable protein mixture takes this appetizer to another level, making it heartier and more delicious. The stuffing can be made ahead and kept refrigerated until needed.

**FOR THE STUFFED PEPPERS**

1 cup TVP (textured vegetable protein) granules, or minced mushrooms

1 tablespoon vegetable oil, plus more for frying

1 teaspoon cumin seeds

½ cup chopped onion

1 tablespoon ginger-garlic paste

1 teaspoon chili powder

1 teaspoon ground cumin

1 teaspoon garam masala

¾ teaspoons salt

1 potato, peeled, cooked, and mashed

½ teaspoon chaat masala

½ teaspoon amchur powder

¼ cup chopped fresh cilantro

8 jalapeño peppers

Green chutney and sweet chutney, for serving

**FOR THE BATTER**

1½ cups chickpea flour (besan)

1 teaspoon chili powder

1 teaspoon ground cumin

1 teaspoon garam masala

1 teaspoon ground coriander

1 teaspoon ground turmeric

1 teaspoon salt

1 tablespoon hot vegetable oil

**TO MAKE THE STUFFED PEPPERS**

1. In a microwave-safe bowl, combine the TVP granules and 1½ cups of water and microwave for 6 minutes (or follow the instructions on the package).

2. Heat 1 tablespoon of oil in a medium kadhai and temper the cumin seeds.

3. Once the seeds crackle, add the onion and ginger-garlic paste. Sauté over medium heat until the onion turns translucent.

4. Add the cooked TVP, chili powder, ground cumin, garam masala, and salt. Mix and cook for 5 minutes.

5. Transfer the TVP mixture to a bowl. Add the mashed potato, chaat masala, amchur powder, and cilantro. Mix well.

6. Partially slit the jalapeños and remove all the seeds. Stuff each jalapeño with a generous amount of the prepared stuffing and set aside.

**TO MAKE THE BATTER**

7. In a bowl, prepare the batter by combining the chickpea flour, chili powder, cumin, garam masala, coriander, turmeric, and salt.

8. Gradually add up to 1½ cups of water to make a lump-free, thick-coating batter. Stir the hot oil into the batter.

9. Pour some oil for frying into a medium kadhai over medium heat. Working in batches, dip the stuffed jalapeños in the batter, coat them well, transfer them to the kadhai, and fry them evenly until they turn golden.

10. Serve hot with green chutney and sweet chutney.

VARIATION TIP: If you like, you can skip the batter and shallow-fry the stuffed jalapeños.

PER SERVING (1 STUFFED PEPPER): Calories: 150; Total fat: 5g; Saturated fat: 0g; Sodium: 545mg; Carbohydrates: 21g; Sugar: 4g; Fiber: 4g; Protein: 6g

# Chatpata Fruit Salad
# (Sweet and Spicy Fruit Salad)

**PREP TIME:** 15 minutes • **SERVES 4**

Chatpata fruit salad is a part of Indian street food cuisine. *Chatpata* means it showcases myriad flavors—sweet, savory, and tangy—all at once. This salad is a fun way to enjoy fruits in a nontraditional way. To save time, you can purchase prechopped fruit, but cutting them fresh yourself will give you the best result.

1 apple, cored and coarsely chopped

1 banana, sliced

2 cups chopped mixed fruits (such as mango, blueberries, pineapple, kiwi, cantaloupe)

2 tablespoons pomegranate seeds

½ teaspoon amchur powder

½ teaspoon black salt

½ teaspoon ground cumin

½ teaspoon chaat masala

¼ teaspoon freshly ground black pepper

1 tablespoon chopped fresh mint

1. Combine the apple, banana, mixed fruits, and pomegranate seeds in a large bowl.

2. Add the amchur powder, black salt, cumin, chaat masala, pepper, and mint.

3. Mix it all together and serve, or cover and chill in the refrigerator until ready to serve.

**VARIATION TIP:** This fruit salad is very customizable. Add any fruits you have on hand. You can also add some nuts or seeds for extra crunch.

PER SERVING: Calories: 105; Total fat: 1g; Saturated fat: 0g; Sodium: 293mg; Carbohydrates: 27g; Sugar: 20g; Fiber: 3g; Protein: 1g

# Vangyacha Kaap
# (Crispy Fried Eggplant)

**PREP TIME:** 5 minutes, plus 30 minutes to marinate • **COOK TIME:** 5 minutes

**SERVES 6**

This crispy snack is from Maharashtrian cuisine. It is an easy and delicious way to cook eggplant. The result looks like bacon strips. You can serve them as an appetizer or snack, or use as a garnish. Look for an eggplant variety that has fewer seeds.

½ cup chili powder

3 tablespoons salt

1 (10-ounce) eggplant, thinly sliced

1 cup chickpea flour (besan)

⅓ cup rice flour

1 teaspoon ground coriander

1 teaspoon ground cumin

Vegetable oil, for frying

1. Combine the chili powder and salt in a shallow dish. Set aside 1 tablespoon of this mixture.

2. Dip the eggplant slices into the dish to coat both sides with the mixture. Transfer it to a bowl and set aside to marinate for 30 minutes.

3. Meanwhile, in a separate bowl, combine the chickpea flour, rice flour, coriander, cumin, and reserved chili powder and salt mixture.

4. After 30 minutes, coat both sides of the marinated eggplant slices with the flour mixture.

5. Heat a thin layer of vegetable oil in a pan over medium heat. Add the eggplant strips and fry until golden brown and crisp, about 2 minutes per side. Serve hot.

**VARIATION TIP:** You can also use an air fryer or deep-fry the eggplants for an even crunchier texture.

PER SERVING: Calories: 161; Total fat: 7g; Saturated fat: 1g; Sodium: 1432mg; Carbohydrates: 21g; Sugar: 4g; Fiber: 5g; Protein: 5g

# Hara Bhara Kebab
# (Crispy Green Fritters)

**PREP TIME:** 15 minutes • **COOK TIME:** 40 minutes • **MAKES 25 KEBABS**

This starter is a restaurant favorite. These kebabs are soft inside and crispy on the outside. The melt-in-your-mouth bite-size appetizers are perfect for when you have guests over and are a great vegan alternative to kebabs made with meat. Blanching the spinach helps retain the green color.

---

5 ounces spinach

2 teaspoons salt, divided

2 tablespoons vegetable oil, plus more for shallow frying

1 teaspoon cumin seeds

1 tablespoon ginger-garlic paste

3 green chile peppers, finely chopped

1 green bell pepper (any color), finely chopped

½ cup green peas

1 teaspoon ground turmeric

6 fresh mint leaves

½ cup fresh cilantro leaves

4 potatoes, peeled, cooked, and mashed

1 teaspoon black salt

1 teaspoon ground cumin

1 teaspoon garam masala

1 teaspoon amchur powder

---

1. Fill a medium pot with water and bring to a boil. Fill a bowl with ice cubes and cold water.

2. Add the spinach and 1 teaspoon of salt to the boiling water and let the spinach blanch for 2 minutes. Using tongs or a slotted spoon, transfer the spinach to the ice bath and let it sit for 2 minutes. Drain the spinach, transfer to another bowl. and set aside.

3. In a medium pan, heat the oil and sauté the cumin seeds, ginger-garlic paste, and green chiles. Add the bell pepper, peas, turmeric, and blanched spinach and sauté until the liquid evaporates, about 15 minutes. Take the pan off the heat and allow the contents to cool.

4. Once cool, transfer the contents of the pan to a food processor, add the mint and cilantro, and process to a smooth paste. Transfer the paste to a medium bowl.

5. Add the mashed potatoes, black salt, ground cumin, garam masala, amchur powder, and remaining 1 teaspoon of salt and mix everything well together.

6. Shape the paste into about 25 balls and flatten them gently into patties.

7. Heat some oil in a pan and shallow-fry each patty evenly until golden brown and a little crispy. The insides will remain soft.

8. Transfer the patties to a plate lined with paper towels to absorb any excess oil.

VARIATION TIP: You can use baby spinach or mixed greens in place of the spinach. Instead of frying, you can bake these kebabs at 350°F for 25 to 30 minutes.

PER SERVING (5 KEBABS): Calories: 221; Total fat: 6g; Saturated fat: 1g; Sodium: 1123mg; Carbohydrates: 37g; Sugar: 4g; Fiber: 6g; Protein: 6g

# Sweet Potato Tikki

**PREP TIME:** 25 minutes • **COOK TIME:** 10 minutes • **MAKES 15 TIKKIS**

This recipe is a take on the very famous aloo tikki, which is a North Indian street food similar to hash browns. *Aloo* means "potatoes" and *tikki* means "patties" or "cutlets." Here, sweet potato is mixed with regular potatoes to create a tempting party appetizer. The texture is buttery-soft on the inside and crisp on the outside.

1 sweet potato, peeled, cooked, and mashed

2 potatoes, peeled, cooked, and mashed

2 green chile peppers, minced

3 tablespoons finely chopped fresh cilantro

1 tablespoon ginger paste

1 tablespoon garlic paste

1 teaspoon ground cumin

1 teaspoon chili powder

1 teaspoon salt

½ teaspoon ground turmeric

1 cup bread crumbs

2 tablespoons vegetable oil

Green chutney and sweet chutney, for serving

1. Combine the mashed potatoes in a large bowl.

2. Add the green chiles, cilantro, ginger paste, garlic paste, cumin, chili powder, salt, and turmeric. Mix it all together until it forms a soft dough. There is no need to knead it; just mix it all together until well combined.

3. Shape the dough into 15 equal balls. Flatten each one lightly into a patty.

4. Pour the bread crumbs into a shallow bowl. Coat the tikkis with the bread crumbs.

5. Heat a pan over medium heat, then pour in the oil. Working in batches, fry the tikkis for 2 minutes or until crisp, then flip them and cook the other side for another 2 minutes or so.

6. Transfer to a plate lined with paper towels to absorb any excess oil. Serve with green chutney and sweet chutney.

PER SERVING (3 TIKKIS): Calories: 215; Total fat: 7g; Saturated fat: 1g; Sodium: 621mg; Carbohydrates: 35g; Sugar: 4g; Fiber: 4g; Protein: 5g

# Cauliflower 65 (Crispy Cauliflower Florets)

**PREP TIME:** 20 minutes • **COOK TIME:** 40 minutes • **SERVES 4**

This crispy, crunchy cauliflower is a vegan take on Chicken 65, which is a popular starter in India. This recipe works great with broccoli, too.

2 teaspoons salt, divided

½ teaspoon ground turmeric

1 cauliflower head, cut into florets

2 tablespoons cornstarch

¼ cup all-purpose flour

¼ cup chickpea flour (besan)

2 tablespoons rice flour

1 teaspoon garam masala

2 tablespoons chopped fresh curry leaves

2 tablespoons chili-garlic sauce

Vegetable oil, for frying

1 tablespoon chaat masala

Chutney, for serving

1. Fill a medium pot with water and add 1 teaspoon of salt and the turmeric. Bring the water to a boil over medium heat.

2. Add the cauliflower florets and cook for 15 minutes or until cooked but still firm. They need to hold their shape when being fried.

3. Drain the florets and run them under cold water to stop the cooking process. Transfer to a medium bowl.

4. Add the cornstarch to the bowl and coat the florets well. Set aside.

5. In a separate bowl, combine the all-purpose flour, chickpea flour, rice flour, garam masala, curry leaves, chili-garlic sauce, and 1 teaspoon of salt.

6. Gradually add ¾ cup of water to make a thick batter of pouring consistency.

7. Toss the cauliflower florets in the batter to coat them well.

8. In a large pan, heat some oil over medium heat. When the oil is hot, deep-fry the florets in batches until golden and crisp.

9. Transfer the fried florets to a paper towel–lined plate to soak up the excess oil. Sprinkle the florets with the chaat masala and mix.

PER SERVING: Calories: 191; Total fat: 8g; Saturated fat: 1g; Sodium: 744mg; Carbohydrates: 25g; Sugar: 4g; Fiber: 5g; Protein: 6g

# Paruppu Vadai (Lentil Fritters)

**PREP TIME:** 15 minutes, plus 2 hours to soak • **COOK TIME:** 20 minutes

**MAKES 30 VADAIS**

Paruppu vadai is a popular street food from South Indian cuisine. *Paruppu* means "lentils" and *vadai* means "fritters." This is a fried appetizer or snack that's prepared on auspicious and happy occasions, such as weddings and festivals.

| | | |
|---|---|---|
| 1 cup chana dal | ½ teaspoon asafetida (hing) | 1 teaspoon salt |
| ½ cup tur dal | 10 dried red chiles | ⅓ cup finely chopped fresh cilantro |
| ¼ cup urad dal | 8 fresh curry leaves | Vegetable oil, for frying |

1. Put the chana dal, tur dal, and urad dal in a large bowl, cover with water, and soak for 2 hours.

2. Drain the water and transfer the dal mixture to a food processor. Add the asafetida, red chiles, curry leaves, and salt and process to a coarse paste. Add up to 3 tablespoons of water if necessary to achieve the correct consistency. Add the cilantro and mix well.

3. Shape the mixture into golf ball–size balls and flatten each one slightly into a disk.

4. Heat some oil for deep-frying in a medium kadhai over low heat.

5. When the oil is hot, add 1 to 3 vadais and deep-fry on each side for about 3 minutes. Keep turning them to make sure both sides get evenly fried.

6. Transfer the vadais to a paper towel–lined plate to soak up any excess oil.

**INGREDIENT TIP:** Add ½ cup of chopped onion to the batter along with the cilantro for more crunch and flavor.

PER SERVING (3 VADAIS): Calories: 147; Total fat: 3g; Saturated fat: 0g; Sodium: 238mg; Carbohydrates: 22g; Sugar: 3g; Fiber: 8g; Protein: 8g

# Chile Cheese Corn Toast

**PREP TIME:** 15 minutes • **COOK TIME:** 5 minutes • **MAKES 12 TOASTS**

This mouthwatering street food from Mumbai is a fun, cheesy bread dish packed with flavorful veggies and spices. This recipe calls for all kinds of chiles, which makes it spicy, but you can reduce the chiles to your heat preference. You can prep the vegetables and store in the refrigerator until needed.

1 cup sweet corn kernels, thawed if frozen

1 bell pepper (any color), finely chopped

½ cup finely chopped onion

2 green chile peppers, minced

6 garlic cloves, minced

1 tablespoon red pepper flakes

1½ teaspoons dried oregano or mixed herbs

1 teaspoon ground cumin

1 teaspoon chaat masala

1 teaspoon chili powder

½ teaspoon salt

½ teaspoon freshly ground black pepper

1 cup grated vegan cheddar cheese, divided

¼ cup chopped fresh cilantro

6 bread slices

⅓ cup vegan cream cheese

½ cup green chutney

1 teaspoon black salt

1. In a large bowl, combine the sweet corn, bell pepper, onion, green chiles, garlic, red pepper flakes, oregano, cumin, chaat masala, chili powder, salt, and black pepper. Mix well. Add ½ cup of cheese and the cilantro. Mix again and set aside.

2. Lightly toast the bread slices. Layer the slices with the cream cheese, followed by the green chutney. Sprinkle black salt on each slice.

3. Spread the veggie mixture on top. Top with the remaining ½ cup of cheese.

4. Place the bread slices in a pan over medium heat. Cover and cook until the cheese melts.

PER SERVING (1 TOAST): Calories: 145; Total fat: 5g; Saturated fat: 3g; Sodium: 623mg; Carbohydrates: 21g; Sugar: 8g; Fiber: 3g; Protein: 7g

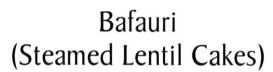

# Bafauri
# (Steamed Lentil Cakes)

**PREP TIME:** 15 minutes, plus 4 hours to soak • **COOK TIME:** 15 minutes
**MAKES 6 CAKES**

Bafauri is a lentil dish from Bhojpuri cuisine. A healthy alternative to fried pakoras, it's low in calories, high in protein, vegan, and delicious!

1 cup chana dal

2 green chile peppers, finely chopped

1 cup finely chopped onion

2 tablespoons chopped fresh cilantro

1 teaspoon ginger-garlic paste

1 teaspoon ground turmeric

1 teaspoon chili powder

1 teaspoon carom seeds (optional)

1 teaspoon salt

Green chutney, for serving

1. Put the chana dal in a small bowl, cover with water, and soak for 4 hours. Drain.

2. Transfer the dal to a mixer grinder. Add ¼ cup of fresh water and grind to a thick, coarse paste. It should not be pourable. Transfer the paste to a medium bowl. Add the green chiles, onion, cilantro, ginger-garlic paste, turmeric, chili powder, carom seeds (if using), and salt. Mix everything well together.

3. Divide the mixture into 6 equal balls and flatten each one into a patty.

4. Pour 1 inch of water into a pot or idli cooker over medium heat, and place a steamer basket in the pot. Place the patties in the steamer basket and steam for 12 minutes. (If using an idli cooker, spray the molds with nonstick cooking spray and place a patty in each mold.)

5. Serve with green chutney.

VARIATION TIP: After the bafauri are steamed, you can shallow-fry them for a crispier texture and flavor.

PER SERVING (1 CAKE): Calories: 135; Total fat: 1g; Saturated fat: 0g; Sodium: 408mg; Carbohydrates: 25g; Sugar: 5g; Fiber: 9g; Protein: 9g

# Bread Upma

**PREP TIME:** 10 minutes • **COOK TIME:** 10 minutes • **SERVES 6**

Upma is a South Indian dish similar to porridge and usually made with semolina and veggies. There are many variations of this recipe, and bread upma is one such variation. It's a delicious dish that's made with leftover bread (or leftover rice). Serve for breakfast or as an evening snack.

2 tablespoons vegetable oil

1 teaspoon mustard seeds

1 teaspoon cumin seeds

1 tablespoon urad dal

6 fresh curry leaves

4 green chile peppers, minced

1 cup finely chopped onion

2 tomatoes, finely chopped

1 bell pepper (any color), finely chopped

1½ teaspoons salt, divided

1 teaspoon ground turmeric

22 white bread slices, torn into croutons

¼ cup chopped fresh cilantro

1 tablespoon freshly squeezed lemon juice

1. Heat the oil in a large kadhai. Temper the mustard seeds and cumin seeds. Once they crackle, add the urad dal, curry leaves, and green chiles. Sauté until the lentils turn light golden.

2. Add the onion and sauté until translucent. Add the tomatoes, bell pepper, and 1 teaspoon of salt. Stir and cook until the tomatoes turn soft and pulpy.

3. Add the turmeric, fry for 15 seconds, and then add the bread pieces. Carefully mix it all together and cook until the bread softens and shrinks.

4. Add the cilantro, lemon juice, and remaining ½ teaspoon of salt. Mix well and take the kadhai off the heat.

**INGREDIENT TIP:** Although white bread slices are preferred, you can use any kind of bread for this recipe.

PER SERVING: Calories: 327; Total fat: 7g; Saturated fat: 1g; Sodium: 1079mg; Carbohydrates: 54g; Sugar: 10g; Fiber: 12g; Protein: 13g

# Puff Pastry Samosas

**PREP TIME:** 15 minutes • **COOK TIME:** 30 minutes • **MAKES 9 SAMOSAS**

This popular North Indian recipe makes a fun and tasty baked snack for all. Use potatoes that are high in starch, such as Yukon Gold or russets.

---

1 tablespoon
  vegetable oil

1 teaspoon cumin seeds

1 tablespoon
  ginger-garlic paste

1 cup minced
  mushrooms

¼ cup green peas

3 green chile
  peppers, minced

2 tablespoons chopped
  fresh cilantro

1 teaspoon ground
  turmeric

1 teaspoon
  ground cumin

1 teaspoon ground
  coriander

2 teaspoons
  garam masala

1 teaspoon
  amchur powder

2 potatoes, peeled,
  cooked, and mashed

1 teaspoon salt

1 frozen puff pastry
  sheet or phyllo
  sheet, thawed

Green chutney
  for serving

---

1. Preheat the oven to 450°F. Line a rimmed baking sheet with parchment paper.

2. Heat the oil in a pan over medium heat. Add the cumin seeds. Once they crackle, add the ginger-garlic paste. Sauté for 30 seconds. Add the mushrooms and cook until the moisture evaporates, 6 to 7 minutes. Add the green peas, green chiles, and cilantro and fry for 1 minute.

3. Add the turmeric, ground cumin, coriander, garam masala, and amchur powder and fry for 1 minute.

4. Stir in the mashed potatoes and salt. Cook for 1 minute, then remove the pan from the heat and allow to cool.

5. Cut the pastry sheet into 9 squares. Place 1 tablespoon of potato mixture in the center of each pastry square. Fold to make a triangle. Press the edges with a fork to seal them. Transfer to the prepared baking sheet.

6. Bake for 20 minutes or until they puff up and turn golden brown.

7. Let them cool for a minute, then serve with green chutney and sweet chutney.

PER SERVING (1 SAMOSA): Calories: 221; Total fat: 13g; Saturated fat: 3g; Sodium: 335mg; Carbohydrates: 24g; Sugar: 2g; Fiber: 2g; Protein: 4g

# Indian Trail Mix

**PREP TIME:** 5 minutes • **COOK TIME:** 10 minutes • **MAKES 10 CUPS**

Using Rice Krispies makes this crispy, savory snack a quick fix when you have a craving for something crunchy. Make a large batch and store it in an airtight container. It stays fresh for 3 to 4 weeks.

---

2 tablespoons
   vegetable oil

1 teaspoon
   mustard seeds

1 teaspoon cumin seeds

¼ teaspoon
   asafetida (hing)

10 to 12 fresh
   curry leaves

2 serrano peppers,
   finely chopped

¼ cup cashews

¼ cup peanuts

¼ cup daliya

1 teaspoon chili powder

1 teaspoon ground
   turmeric

12 ounces unsweetened
   Rice Krispies

1 teaspoon salt

1 teaspoon black salt

---

1. Pour the oil into a medium kadhai. Wait until the oil is hot enough to temper. Add the mustard seeds and cumin seeds and temper them. Add the asafetida, curry leaves, and serrano peppers. Sauté until the peppers become fragrant. Add the cashews, peanuts, and daliya. Fry for 2 minutes or until the cashews and peanuts turn slightly brown. Add the chili powder and turmeric and sauté for another 2 minutes. Add the Rice Krispies and salt and mix everything together well.

2. Take the kadhai off the heat. Add the black salt.

PER SERVING (1 CUP): Calories: 200; Total fat: 7g; Saturated fat: 1g; Sodium: 514mg; Carbohydrates: 31g; Sugar: 4g; Fiber: 1g; Protein: 4g

# Tomato (Eggless) Omelet

**PREP TIME:** 15 minutes, plus 15 minutes to rest • **COOK TIME:** 45 minutes

**MAKES 6 PANCAKES**

Like a frittata, this is a popular eggless omelet that can be served for breakfast or as an evening snack. Loaded with veggies, these thick pancakes are as nutritious as they are delicious.

---

1 cup chickpea flour (besan)

¼ cup rice flour

1 teaspoon salt

⅓ cup plain unsweetened almond milk yogurt

1⅓ cups finely chopped onion, divided

1 cup tomato puree

2 green chile peppers, minced

1 bell pepper (any color), chopped

¼ cup plus 2 tablespoons chopped fresh cilantro, divided

1 teaspoon ajwain (optional)

1 teaspoon cumin seeds

1 teaspoon chili powder

1 teaspoon ground turmeric

1 tablespoon grated fresh ginger

¼ teaspoon asafetida (hing)

2 tablespoons ketchup, plus more for serving

½ teaspoon baking soda

1 tablespoon vegetable oil, plus more for frying

1 tomato, finely chopped, for topping

Grated vegan cheese (optional)

Toasted bread and green chutney, for serving

---

1. In a large bowl, combine the chickpea flour, rice flour, salt, ¾ cup of water, and the yogurt. Stir to form a thick batter. Let it rest for 15 minutes.

2. Add 1 cup of onion, the tomato puree, green chiles, bell pepper, and ¼ cup of cilantro. Stir.

3. Add the ajwain (if using), cumin seeds, chili powder, turmeric, ginger, asafetida, ketchup, baking soda, and 1 tablespoon of oil. Stir in ⅓ cup of water gradually to form a thick, flowing batter.

4. In a separate bowl, combine the remaining ⅓ cup of onion, remaining 2 tablespoons of cilantro, and chopped tomato to make the topping.

5. Heat a tawa or skillet over medium heat. Smear the tawa with oil. Pour in a ladleful of batter and spread it out into a thick pancake. Drizzle oil around it.

6. Sprinkle the pancake with some of the topping. Add cheese (if using). Cover the tawa and cook for 3 to 4 minutes. Flip the pancake and cook for another 3 to 4 minutes. Transfer to a plate.

7. Repeat steps 5 and 6 to make as many pancakes as you need.

8. Serve with toasted bread, tomato topping, and green chutney.

PREP TIP: Store any remaining batter in a covered container in the refrigerator for up to 5 days.

PER SERVING (1 PANCAKE): Calories: 202; Total fat: 9g; Saturated fat: 1g; Sodium: 536mg; Carbohydrates: 26g; Sugar: 8g; Fiber: 5g; Protein: 6g

# Indian Curry Pasta

**PREP TIME:** 15 minutes • **COOK TIME:** 15 minutes • **SERVES 6**

This no-sauce pasta is loaded with veggies and can be enjoyed as a snack or a salad. Serve with warm garlic bread.

8 ounces penne pasta

2 tablespoons vegan butter

1 teaspoon mustard seeds

1 teaspoon cumin seeds

6 fresh curry leaves

1 tablespoon ginger-garlic paste

3 green chile peppers, minced

1 cup chopped onion

1 tomato, chopped

1 teaspoon salt

1 cup sliced mushrooms

⅓ cup green peas

1 bell pepper (any color), chopped

1 teaspoon ground turmeric

1 teaspoon ground cumin

1 teaspoon garam masala

1 teaspoon red pepper flakes

½ tablespoon oregano

¼ cup chopped fresh cilantro

1 tablespoon freshly squeezed lemon juice

1. Cook the pasta according to the package instructions. Drain and set aside.

2. Heat the butter in a pan over medium heat. Once the butter melts, temper the mustard seeds and cumin seeds.

3. As they begin to crackle, add the curry leaves, ginger-garlic paste, green chiles, and onion. Fry until the onion turns translucent. Add the tomato and salt and continue to sauté until the tomatoes are cooked. Stir in the mushrooms and sauté for 6 minutes or until the moisture has evaporated. Add the green peas and bell pepper and cook for 2 more minutes. Stir in the turmeric, ground cumin, garam masala, red pepper flakes, and oregano.

4. Add the cooked pasta. Mix it all together so the pasta gets coated well with the masala. Garnish with the cilantro and lemon juice.

**VARIATION TIP:** Garnish the dish with nutritional yeast or vegan Parmesan cheese if you want a cheesier flavor. If you want, add white or red pasta sauce.

PER SERVING: Calories: 224; Total fat: 5g; Saturated fat: 1g; Sodium: 441mg; Carbohydrates: 39g; Sugar: 5g; Fiber: 4g; Protein: 7g

# Chatpati Shakarkandi Chaat (Sweet Potato Chaat)

**PREP TIME:** 40 minutes • **SERVES 4**

This dish is an extremely popular street food snack combining tanginess, spice, sweet, and sour to produce a mouthwatering result. Enjoy this chaat as a snack or as a salad. You can use any combination of sweet potatoes and regular potatoes.

2 potatoes, cooked, peeled, and cut into medium cubes

2 sweet potatoes, cooked, peeled, and cut into medium cubes

6 garlic cloves, minced

½ cup chopped fresh cilantro, divided

1 tablespoon red pepper flakes

1 teaspoon black salt

1 teaspoon freshly ground black pepper

1 tablespoon olive oil

3 tablespoons vegan ghee or butter

1 cup chopped onion

1 teaspoon chaat masala

1 teaspoon amchur powder

1 teaspoon ground cumin

1 teaspoon chili powder

3 tablespoons sweet chutney or 1 tablespoon sugar

3 tablespoons green chutney

1 tablespoon freshly squeezed lemon juice

1. Combine the potatoes and sweet potatoes in a large bowl.

2. Add the garlic, ¼ cup of cilantro, the red pepper flakes, black salt, black pepper, and oil. Stir to coat the potatoes with the dressing.

3. Heat the ghee in a pan over medium heat, then, working in batches, fry the potatoes until golden and crisp, tossing often. As they are cooked, transfer them to another large bowl.

4. Add the onion, chaat masala, amchur, cumin, chili powder, sweet chutney, and green chutney. Mix well.

5. Garnish with the remaining ¼ cup of cilantro and lemon juice. Serve immediately or refrigerate and serve chilled.

PER SERVING: Calories: 303; Total fat: 12g; Saturated fat: 2g; Sodium: 912mg; Carbohydrates: 46g; Sugar: 13g; Fiber: 6g; Protein: 4g

Green Lentil Curry
page 59

# Dals, Legumes, and Soups

# Mixed Dal Tadka (Mixed Lentil Stew)

**PREP TIME:** 15 minutes • **COOK TIME:** 10 minutes • **SERVES 4**

Dal tadka is one of the most common and popular lentil-based dishes in North Indian cuisine. This restaurant classic can very easily be made at home using a variety of spices. Indians consider dal rice to be comfort food. If you don't have all the different dals, just make up the quantity with what you have.

⅓ cup masoor dal

2½ tablespoons moong dal

2½ tablespoons tur dal

½ teaspoon ground turmeric

6 garlic cloves, finely chopped

3 green chile peppers, minced

1 teaspoon ginger paste

1 cup finely chopped onion

1 teaspoon chili powder

1 teaspoon ground cumin

1 teaspoon ground coriander

1 teaspoon salt

1 teaspoon vegetable oil

1 teaspoon cumin seeds

6 fresh curry leaves

¼ teaspoon asafetida (hing)

¼ cup chopped fresh cilantro

Jeera Garlic Rice (page 67) or steamed rice, for serving

1. In a pressure cooker, combine the masoor dal, moong dal, tur dal, turmeric, and 3 cups of water.

2. Pressure cook for 3 whistles (about 20 minutes) and set aside. In a large pan, sauté the garlic, green chiles, and ginger paste over medium heat. Add the onion and sauté until translucent. Add the chili powder, ground cumin, coriander, and salt and sauté for 1 minute.

3. Stir in the cooked dal. Add 1 cup of water (or a bit more if the dal is too thick) and bring to a boil. Turn off the heat.

4. In a tadka pan, heat the oil. Temper the cumin seeds, curry leaves, and asafetida. Pour this tempering over the dal.

5. Garnish with the cilantro and serve with rice.

PER SERVING: Calories: 164; Total fat: 2g; Saturated fat: 0g; Sodium: 611mg; Carbohydrates: 29g; Sugar: 5g; Fiber: 8g; Protein: 9g

# Shahjahani Dal (Royal Chickpea Dal)

**PREP TIME:** 10 minutes • **COOK TIME:** 15 minutes • **SERVES 6**

This unique recipe from Moghlai cuisine is a rich and creamy dal that is royal in every way. Serve with a drizzle of cashew cream.

2 (15-ounce) cans chickpeas, drained and rinsed

1 tablespoon vegetable oil

1 teaspoon cumin seeds

½ teaspoon kalonji (optional)

1 bay leaf

4 cloves

1 teaspoon freshly ground black pepper

1 cinnamon stick

1 tablespoon ginger-garlic paste

1 cup finely chopped onion

1 teaspoon ground turmeric

1 teaspoon chili powder

1 teaspoon ground coriander

1 teaspoon ground cumin

1 teaspoon salt

1 (13-ounce) can unsweetened coconut milk

1 teaspoon garam masala

¼ cup finely chopped fresh cilantro

1. In a bowl, mash the chickpeas with 1 cup of water. Set aside.

2. In a kadhai, heat the oil over medium heat and temper the cumin seeds and kalonji (if using).

3. Add the bay leaf, cloves, black pepper, and cinnamon. Sauté for about 30 seconds.

4. Add the ginger-garlic paste and onion. Sauté until translucent.

5. Add the turmeric, chili powder, coriander, ground cumin, and 2 tablespoons of water. Continue to sauté for an additional 2 minutes. Add the mashed chickpeas and salt.

6. Further mash the chickpeas if needed and bring the mixture to a boil. Add the coconut milk and garam masala and cook for 5 minutes.

7. Serve garnished with the cilantro.

PER SERVING: Calories: 293; Total fat: 19g; Saturated fat: 12g; Sodium: 417mg; Carbohydrates: 28g; Sugar: 5g; Fiber: 7g; Protein: 9g

# Tomato Saar
# (Tomato Coconut Stew)

**PREP TIME:** 15 minutes • **COOK TIME:** 25 minutes • **SERVES 4**

This delicious and simple-to-prepare stew comes from Malayali cuisine. *Saar* means "essence," and here, the essence of tomatoes mixed with coconut makes the dish irresistible. Serve with Jeera Garlic Rice (page 67), curd rice, or steamed rice.

---

5 large tomatoes, coarsely chopped

2 cups unsweetened shredded coconut

1½ teaspoons salt, divided

3 cups vegetable broth

2 green chile peppers

1 teaspoon coconut oil

1 teaspoon cumin seeds

3 tablespoons chopped fresh cilantro, divided

1 teaspoon chili powder

---

1. In a pressure cooker, combine the tomatoes, coconut, 1 teaspoon of salt, and the broth. Cook for 3 whistles (about 20 minutes).

2. Once the pressure releases, open the cooker and add the green chiles. Using an immersion blender, pulse to a smooth puree.

3. In a tadka pan, heat the oil over medium heat and temper the cumin seeds. Once they crackle, stir in 1 tablespoon of cilantro and the chili powder and cook for 15 seconds.

4. Pour in the tomato puree, add the remaining ½ teaspoon of salt, and cook for 1 minute.

5. Garnish with the remaining 1 tablespoon of cilantro and serve.

**PREP TIP:** You can also puree the tomato mixture in a regular mixer grinder. The puree should have a thick, flowing consistency.

PER SERVING: Calories: 205; Total fat: 15g; Saturated fat: 13g; Sodium: 914mg; Carbohydrates: 18g; Sugar: 10g; Fiber: 7g; Protein: 4g

# Sindhi Aloo Kadhi

**PREP TIME:** 10 minutes • **COOK TIME:** 20 minutes • **SERVES 4**

Kadhi is a thick gravy made with chickpea flour and yogurt, but sindhi kadhi is made without yogurt. Be attentive while roasting the chickpea flour because it can burn quickly. Keep the heat low and keep stirring it.

3 tablespoons vegetable oil

¼ teaspoon asafetida (hing)

1 teaspoon mustard seeds

1 teaspoon cumin seeds

5 fenugreek seeds

6 fresh curry leaves

2 green chile peppers, minced

1 teaspoon grated ginger

¼ cup chickpea flour (besan)

1 teaspoon chili powder

1 teaspoon ground turmeric

1 teaspoon salt

2 tomatoes, pureed

2 cups vegetable broth

2 potatoes, cut into cubes

1 tablespoon tamarind paste

¼ cup chopped fresh cilantro

Jeera Garlic Rice (page 67) or steamed rice, for serving

1. In a medium kadhai, heat the oil over medium heat. Temper the asafetida, mustard seeds, cumin seeds, and fenugreek seeds. Once the seeds crackle, add the curry leaves, green chiles, and ginger.

2. Add the chickpea flour, lower the heat, and roast just until it turns light brown.

3. Add the chili powder, turmeric, salt, tomato puree, and broth and cook for 3 minutes.

4. Add the potatoes, cover the kadhai, and cook until the potatoes are soft and cooked.

5. Stir in the tamarind paste and cook for another 2 minutes.

6. Garnish with the cilantro and serve with rice.

PER SERVING: Calories: 231; Total fat: 11g; Saturated fat: 1g; Sodium: 618mg; Carbohydrates: 29g; Sugar: 5g; Fiber: 5g; Protein: 5g

# Arachuvitta Sambhar
# (South Indian Thick Lentil Stew)

**PREP TIME:** 15 minutes • **COOK TIME:** 30 minutes • **SERVES 6**

This is a foolproof version of the popular recipe arachuvitta sambhar, which hails from the Tamil Nadu. It's an aromatic and comforting thick stew prepared with lentils, veggies, and freshly ground coconut paste. If you have other veggies on hand, such as pumpkin, okra, or eggplant, add them along with the tomatoes. Serve this stew with rice.

¼ cup tur dal

½ teaspoon ground turmeric, divided

2 teaspoons coconut oil, divided

2 dried red chile peppers

2 tablespoons urad dal

2 tablespoons chana dal

1 tablespoon coriander seeds

¾ cup unsweetened shredded coconut

2 tablespoons tamarind paste

2 tomatoes, chopped

1 tablespoon sambhar powder or Madras curry powder (optional)

1½ teaspoons salt

½ teaspoon asafetida, divided

5 tablespoons chopped fresh cilantro, divided

1 teaspoon mustard seeds

6 curry leaves

5 fenugreek seeds

1. In a pressure cooker, combine the tur dal, ¼ teaspoon of turmeric, and 1 cup of water. Cook for 3 whistles (about 20 minutes). Mash the cooked dal. Set aside.

2. Heat 1 teaspoon of oil in a pan over medium heat. Add the red chiles, urad dal, chana dal, and coriander seeds and roast for about 4 minutes. Transfer to a bowl and allow to cool.

3. Once cool, transfer the mixture to a mixer grinder, add the shredded coconut and ½ cup of water and grind to a smooth paste. Set aside.

4. In a stockpot over medium heat, combine 4½ cups of water, the tamarind paste, tomatoes, sambhar powder (if using), salt, ¼ teaspoon of asafetida, and remaining ¼ teaspoon of turmeric. Bring to a boil; this will take around 20 minutes.

5. Add the ground coconut paste. Mix well and ensure there are no lumps. Add up to ½ cup of water if it's too thick.

6. Once it returns to a boil, add the mashed lentils. Mix well and remove from the heat after a minute. Garnish with 4 tablespoons of cilantro.

7. Heat the remaining 1 teaspoon of oil in a tadka pan. When the oil is hot, temper the mustard seeds. Once they begin to crackle, add the remaining ¼ teaspoon of asafetida, the curry leaves, fenugreek seeds, and remaining 1 tablespoon of cilantro. Fry for 30 seconds, then pour this tadka over the sambhar.

VARIATION TIP: You can make this sambhar without the ground coconut paste. It will have a thinner consistency.

PER SERVING: Calories: 127; Total fat: 6g; Saturated fat: 5g; Sodium: 589mg; Carbohydrates: 16g; Sugar: 3g; Fiber: 4g; Protein: 5g

# Golyachi Amti
# (Chickpea Flour Balls in Spicy Gravy)

**PREP TIME:** 15 minutes • **COOK TIME:** 40 minutes • **SERVES 4**

Golyachi amti is a unique stew from Maharashtrian cuisine. Here, the chickpea flour balls are cooked in a spicy and tangy tomato-based gravy. Serve amti with bhakri, or rice and zunka.

**FOR THE CHICKPEA FLOUR BALLS**

5 tablespoons chickpea flour (besan)

1 tablespoon chopped fresh cilantro

1 teaspoon vegetable oil

1 teaspoon garlic paste

1 teaspoon salt

1 teaspoon chili powder

½ teaspoon ground cumin

½ teaspoon ground coriander

½ teaspoon ground turmeric

**FOR THE GRAVY**

3 tablespoons vegetable oil

½ cup finely chopped onion

½ tablespoon ginger-garlic paste

¼ teaspoon asafetida (hing)

2 tablespoons finely chopped fresh cilantro

2 tomatoes, finely chopped

3 tablespoons unsweetened shredded coconut

1 teaspoon ground turmeric

2 tablespoons peanut powder

2 teaspoons chili powder

1 teaspoon salt

**TO MAKE THE CHICKPEA FLOUR BALLS**

1. In a medium bowl, combine the chickpea flour, cilantro, 1 tablespoon of water, oil, garlic paste, salt, chili powder, cumin, coriander, and turmeric.

2. Knead the mixture to make a dough. Shape the dough into 12 small balls and set aside while you prepare the gravy.

**TO MAKE THE GRAVY**

3. Heat the oil in a pan over medium heat. Add the onion, ginger-garlic paste, asafetida, and cilantro. Sauté until the onion turns translucent.

4. Add the tomatoes, coconut, and turmeric and sauté until the oil separates.

5. Stir in 2½ cups of warm water, peanut powder, chili powder, and salt.

6. Add the chickpea flour balls and cover the pan.

7. Cook, still over medium heat, for 25 minutes. Once the balls are cooked, they will begin to float in the gravy. To check if the balls are fully cooked, cut one with a spoon. If you're able to cut it easily, it's done; otherwise cook for another 5 minutes and check again.

INGREDIENT TIP: Use freshly shredded coconut if possible. Otherwise, use unsweetened dried coconut.

PER SERVING: Calories: 223; Total fat: 17g; Saturated fat: 3g; Sodium: 1280mg; Carbohydrates: 15g; Sugar: 5g; Fiber: 4g; Protein: 5g

# Rajma Masala (Red Kidney Bean Gravy)

**PREP TIME:** 10 minutes, plus overnight to soak • **COOK TIME:** 1 hour • **SERVES 6**

Rajma masala is a popular restaurant-style recipe. This Punjabi curry made with red kidney beans is aromatic, lightly spiced, creamy, delicious, and nutritious. No wonder many people consider it to be comfort food.

13 ounces dried red kidney beans, soaked overnight and drained

2 teaspoons salt, divided

1 teaspoon ground turmeric, divided

⅓ cup moong dal

3 teaspoons vegetable oil, divided

½ cup coarsely chopped onion

5 garlic cloves, coarsely chopped

1 inch fresh ginger, minced

1 tomato, coarsely chopped

12 almonds

1 teaspoon cumin seeds

1 bay leaf

1 cinnamon stick

2 teaspoons chili powder

1 teaspoon ground coriander

1 teaspoon ground cumin

1 teaspoon garam masala

2 teaspoons crushed kasuri methi (optional)

⅓ cup finely chopped fresh cilantro

1.  In a pressure cooker, combine the soaked beans, 4 cups of water, 1 teaspoon of salt, and ½ teaspoon of turmeric. Pressure cook for 4 whistles (about 25 minutes).

2.  Wait until the pressure releases, then transfer the beans to a bowl and set aside.

3.  Combine the moong dal, remaining ½ teaspoon of turmeric, and 1½ cups of water in the pressure cooker. Pressure cook for 2 whistles (about 15 minutes) and set aside.

4.  Heat 2 teaspoons of oil in a pan over medium heat. Add the onion, garlic, and ginger and sauté until the onion turns translucent.

5.  Add the tomato, the almonds, and the remaining 1 teaspoon of salt. Sauté until the tomato turns soft and pulpy, about 3 minutes.

6. Take the pan off the heat and allow the contents to cool.

7. Once cool, transfer the contents to a mixer grinder and add half the moong dal. Grind to a smooth paste and set aside.

8. In a tadka pan, heat the remaining 1 teaspoon of oil over medium heat. Temper the cumin seeds, bay leaf, and cinnamon.

9. Add the vegetable and nut paste along with ¼ cup of water and cook for 4 minutes or until the oil separates.

10. Stir in the chili powder, coriander, and ground cumin. Add the remaining moong dal and mix everything well. Cook for 1 minute, then add the cooked kidney beans, garam masala, kasuri methi (if using), and cilantro. Mix and cook for 5 minutes.

PREP TIP: If the rajma is too thick, adjust the consistency by slowly adding water and stirring until the desired consistency is achieved.

PER SERVING: Calories: 311; Total fat: 6g; Saturated fat: 4g; Sodium: 814mg; Carbohydrates: 49g; Sugar: 4g; Fiber: 14g; Protein: 18g

# Kathrikai Rasavangi
# (Eggplant Lentil Curry)

**PREP TIME:** 15 minutes • **COOK TIME:** 45 minutes • **SERVES 6**

This is a popular recipe from Tamil Nadu. *Kathrikai* means "eggplant" and *rasavangi* means "gravy" in Tamil. This dish is made on special occasions and is delicious! You can use any eggplant, but keep in mind that the eggplant will shrink when it cooks. This curry is thick, but you can add up to 1 cup of water toward the end of this recipe if you prefer a soupier consistency.

½ cup tur dal

1¼ teaspoons ground turmeric, divided

2 teaspoons vegetable oil, divided

¼ cup chana dal

1 tablespoon coriander seeds

6 dried red chile peppers

1 cup unsweetened shredded coconut

1 (9-ounce) eggplant, cut into cubes

2 tablespoons tamarind paste

2 teaspoons salt

1 teaspoon mustard seeds

¼ teaspoon asafetida (hing)

Steamed rice, for serving

1. In a pressure cooker, combine the tur dal, ¼ teaspoon of turmeric, and 3 cups of water. Cook for 2 whistles (about 15 minutes).

2. Once the pressure releases, transfer the dal to a medium bowl, mash it well, and set aside.

3. In a medium pan over medium heat, heat 1 teaspoon of oil. Sauté the chana dal, coriander, and red chiles until the seeds turn slightly brown, 5 minutes. Transfer to a medium bowl and allow everything to cool.

4. Transfer the contents of the bowl to a food processor. Add the coconut and 1 cup of water and grind to a smooth paste. Set aside.

5. Pour 4 cups of water into a large kadhai, add the eggplant, tamarind paste, and remaining 1 teaspoon of turmeric, and bring to a boil over medium heat.

6. Reduce the heat, cover, and continue to cook until the eggplant is soft, about 15 minutes.

7. Add the coconut paste, salt, and mashed tur dal. Cook for another 10 minutes, then remove from the heat.

8. In a tadka pan, heat the remaining 1 teaspoon of oil. Temper the mustard seeds and asafetida, and pour the tadka on top of the contents of the kadhai.

9. Cover the kadhai to preserve the flavor and aroma. Serve with rice.

PER SERVING: Calories: 172; Total fat: 7g; Saturated fat: 4g; Sodium: 784mg; Carbohydrates: 23g; Sugar: 5g; Fiber: 10g; Protein: 7g

# Jaisalmeri Chana (Black Chickpea Curry)

**PREP TIME:** 15 minutes, plus overnight to soak • **COOK TIME:** 40 minutes • **SERVES 4**

Jaisalmeri chana is a popular recipe from Rajasthani cuisine where black (kala) or brown chickpeas are cooked in a yogurt-based gravy. An easy way to make the dish vegan is to use chickpea flour instead of yogurt. If you don't have kala chana, just use regular chickpeas.

1½ cups kala chana, soaked overnight and drained

3 cups vegetable broth

2 teaspoons salt, divided

1½ teaspoons ground turmeric, divided

3 tablespoons chickpea flour (besan)

1¼ cups plain unsweetened nondairy milk, divided

1 tablespoon vegetable oil

1 teaspoon cumin seeds

¼ teaspoon asafetida (hing)

2 green chile peppers

1 cup finely chopped onion

1 tomato, finely chopped

1 teaspoon chili powder

1 teaspoon ground coriander

1 teaspoon ground cumin

2 tablespoons chopped fresh cilantro

1 teaspoon garam masala

1. In a pressure cooker, combine the soaked kala chana, vegetable broth, 1 teaspoon of salt, and 1 teaspoon of turmeric. Cook them for 4 whistles (about 25 minutes), then drain and set aside.

2. In a small bowl, prepare a slurry by mixing the chickpea flour with ¼ cup of milk until there are no lumps. Set aside.

3. Heat the oil in a medium kadhai over medium heat. Temper the cumin seeds, and, once they begin to crackle, add the asafetida, green chiles, and onion. Sauté until the onion turns translucent. Add the tomato and sauté until soft and pulpy. Add the chili powder, coriander, ground cumin, and remaining ½ teaspoon of turmeric. Bhunao the masala until the oil separates.

4. Add the chickpea flour slurry along with the remaining 1 cup of milk. Mix well.

5. Add the cooked kala chana and remaining 1 teaspoon of salt, stir well, and cook for 5 minutes. Garnish with the cilantro and garam masala.

PER SERVING: Calories: 396; Total fat: 10g; Saturated fat: 4g; Sodium: 655mg; Carbohydrates: 60g; Sugar: 13g; Fiber: 12g; Protein: 20g

# Matki Chi Usal
# (Moth Bean Sprouts Gravy)

**PREP TIME:** 10 minutes • **COOK TIME:** 15 minutes • **SERVES 4**

This spicy, tangy, protein-rich Maharashtrian snack is normally served with dinner rolls, but you can serve it with any Indian flatbread or rice. It's made with moth bean sprouts, but you can use any sprouts you like.

| | | |
|---|---|---|
| 1 onion, coarsely chopped | 1 green chile pepper | 1 teaspoon salt |
| 5 garlic cloves | ½ inch fresh ginger | 1 teaspoon ground turmeric |
| 1½ teaspoons fennel seeds | 1 tablespoon vegetable oil | 1 teaspoon chili powder |
| 1½ teaspoons coriander seeds | 1 teaspoon mustard seeds | 1 cup moth bean sprouts |
| 2 tablespoons unsweetened shredded coconut | 1 teaspoon cumin seeds | 2 tablespoons chopped fresh cilantro |
| | 6 fresh curry leaves | 1½ teaspoons freshly squeezed lemon juice |
| | 1 tomato, chopped | |

1. In a mixer grinder, grind half the onion and the garlic, fennel seeds, coriander seeds, coconut, chile, and ginger to a smooth paste. Set aside.

2. Heat the oil in a pan over medium heat. Temper the mustard seeds and cumin seeds. Once they begin to crackle, add the curry leaves and the rest of the onion. Sauté until the onion turns translucent.

3. Add the tomato and salt and cook until soft. Add the ground onion paste and bhunao for 3 minutes or until the oil separates, then stir in the turmeric and chili powder. Sauté for 30 seconds.

4. Add the sprouts and 2 cups of water. Mix, cover, and cook for 8 minutes.

5. Garnish with the cilantro and lemon juice.

PER SERVING: Calories: 103; Total fat: 5g; Saturated fat: 1g; Sodium: 612mg; Carbohydrates: 13g; Sugar: 3g; Fiber: 3g; Protein: 4g

# Black-Eyed Pea and Dill Curry

**PREP TIME:** 20 minutes, plus overnight to soak • **COOK TIME:** 35 minutes • **SERVES 4**

The tangy flavor of dill works beautifully with these peas to make a fragrant and wholesome dish. Because dill has such a strong flavor, don't be tempted to add more than suggested here to avoid overpowering the dish. Serve with any flatbread, such as bhakri, naan, or roti.

---

1 cup dried black-eyed peas, soaked overnight and drained

1½ teaspoons ground turmeric, divided

1¾ teaspoons salt, divided

1 tablespoon vegetable oil

1 teaspoon mustard seeds

1 teaspoon cumin seeds

6 garlic cloves, sliced

1 tablespoon ginger paste

¼ teaspoon asafetida (hing)

6 curry leaves

1 cup chopped onion

2 green chile peppers, sliced

½ cup fresh dill, coarsely chopped

2 teaspoons freshly squeezed lemon juice

---

1. In a pressure cooker, combine the soaked peas, 2 cups of water, ½ teaspoon of turmeric, and 1 teaspoon of salt. Cook for 4 whistles (about 25 minutes). When the pressure releases, open the cooker, drain the water, and set aside.

2. Heat the oil in a pan over medium heat. Temper the mustard seeds and cumin seeds. Once they begin to crackle, sauté the garlic, ginger, asafetida, and curry leaves for 1 minute.

3. Add the onion and green chiles. Sauté until the onion turns translucent.

4. Stir in the remaining 1 teaspoon of turmeric and the dill. Add 2 tablespoons of water and sauté for 2 minutes.

5. Add the cooked black-eyed peas and the remaining ¾ teaspoon of salt and mix well.

6. Cook for another minute, then stir in the lemon juice.

PER SERVING: Calories: 232; Total fat: 7g; Saturated fat: 1g; Sodium: 832mg; Carbohydrates: 35g; Sugar: 8g; Fiber: 9g; Protein: 10g

# Chatpata Tawa Chole
# (Stir-Fried Chickpeas)

**PREP TIME:** 35 minutes • **COOK TIME:** 10 minutes • **SERVES 4**

Also known as chana chaat, this North Indian street food is bursting with flavor and is a variation on regular chana masala. The dish works as a snack or salad, served with naan or khulcha.

---

2 (15-ounce) cans chickpeas, drained and rinsed

2 tablespoons chole masala

1 teaspoon chili powder

1 teaspoon ground cumin

1 teaspoon garam masala

1 tablespoon vegetable oil

1 teaspoon ajwain (optional)

1 tablespoon ginger-garlic paste

1 cup sliced onions, divided

¾ teaspoon salt

1 tomato, chopped

½ cup chopped bell pepper (any color)

¼ cup chopped fresh cilantro

1 tablespoon freshly squeezed lemon juice

---

1. In a large bowl, combine the chickpeas, chole masala, chili powder, cumin, and garam masala and stir to coat the chickpeas. Set aside for 30 minutes.

2. Heat the oil in a kadhai over medium heat. Fry the ajwain (if using), and once they crackle, add the ginger-garlic paste, ¾ cup of onions, and salt. Sauté until the onion turns translucent.

3. Add the tomato and bell pepper. Sauté until the tomato turns soft.

4. Add the marinated chickpeas, mix it all together, and cook for 5 minutes, then remove from the heat.

5. Garnish with the cilantro, remaining ¼ cup of onion, and the lemon juice.

**INGREDIENT TIP:** If chole masala is not available, increase the garam masala to 1½ teaspoons.

PER SERVING: Calories: 254; Total fat: 7g; Saturated fat: 1g; Sodium: 468mg; Carbohydrates: 37g; Sugar: 8g; Fiber: 11g; Protein: 12g

# Creamy Dal Makhani

**PREP TIME:** 1 hour, plus 4 hours to soak • **COOK TIME:** 1 hour 30 minutes • **SERVES 4**

Dal makhani is the most popular lentil recipe from North Indian cuisine. Slow cooking the lentils is key in order to get the desired restaurant-style rich and creamy texture.

1 cup whole black gram lentils (sabut urad dal)

5 tablespoons vegan butter, divided

1 tablespoon ginger-garlic paste

1 teaspoon chili powder

3 large tomatoes, pureed

1 teaspoon salt, plus more if needed

1 teaspoon kasuri methi (optional)

1 teaspoon garam masala

2 tablespoons cashew cream

Jeera Garlic Rice (page 67), steamed rice, or any Indian flatbread, for serving

1. Rinse the lentils and then soak them in a bowl of water for 4 hours. Drain and transfer to a medium stockpot.

2. Add 3 cups of water and bring to a boil, then lower the heat and cook for 1 hour. Stir frequently, adding up to 1 cup of hot water as necessary and skimming off any froth that collects on the top. When the lentils mash easily, that means they are done. At this point, take the pot off the heat.

3. Heat 1 tablespoon of butter in a kadhai over medium heat. Add the ginger-garlic paste and fry for 1 minute. Add the chili powder and cook until the oil separates. Add the tomato puree and salt. Continue to cook for 4 minutes or until the raw smell of tomato dissipates.

4. Transfer the cooked lentils to the kadhai and stir in 2 tablespoons of butter. Mix well. Continue to cook the dal over low heat for 20 minutes. Add up to ½ cup of hot water if it gets too thick, and add salt if needed.

5. Stir in the kasuri methi (if using), garam masala, cashew cream, and remaining 2 tablespoons of butter. Cook for 5 minutes, then remove from the heat.

6. Serve warm with rice or flatbread.

PER SERVING: Calories: 351; Total fat: 16g; Saturated fat: 4g; Sodium: 728mg; Carbohydrates: 39g; Sugar: 5g; Fiber: 7g; Protein: 14g

# Green Lentil Curry

**PREP TIME:** 10 minutes • **COOK TIME:** 40 minutes • **SERVES 4**

Seasoned with mild spices, this protein-rich dish is well balanced in terms of flavors and is very easy to make. Avoid overcooking the lentils; they should hold their shape.

1⅓ cups dried green lentils

1½ teaspoons salt, divided

1 tablespoon vegetable oil

1 teaspoon mustard seeds

1 teaspoon cumin seeds

¼ teaspoon fenugreek seeds

6 curry leaves

4 dried red chile peppers

¼ teaspoon asafetida (hing)

½ cup chopped onion

1 tablespoon ginger paste

6 garlic cloves, finely chopped

1 tomato, coarsely chopped

1 teaspoon chili powder

1 teaspoon ground coriander

1 teaspoon amchur powder

2 teaspoons chopped fresh cilantro

Roti or naan, for serving

1. Rinse the green lentils under running water, then combine them in a medium pan with 2½ cups of water and 1 teaspoon of salt. Cook over medium heat for about 25 minutes or until al dente, then drain them and set aside.

2. In the same pan, heat the oil over medium heat. Once hot, temper the mustard seeds, cumin seeds, fenugreek seeds, curry leaves, red chiles, and asafetida.

3. Stir in the onion, ginger paste, and garlic. Sauté until translucent.

4. Add the tomato and remaining ½ teaspoon of salt. Cook until the tomato turns soft and pulpy. Add the chili powder, coriander, amchur powder, and lentils and mix everything together well.

5. Cook for 3 minutes and then garnish with the cilantro. Serve with roti or naan.

INGREDIENT TIP: You can make this dish with any lentil variety.

PER SERVING: Calories: 285; Total fat: 5g; Saturated fat: 1g; Sodium: 800mg; Carbohydrates: 46g; Sugar: 3g; Fiber: 8g; Protein: 17g

# Restaurant-Style Tomato Soup

**PREP TIME:** 15 minutes • **COOK TIME:** 40 minutes • **SERVES 4**

Tomato soup is one of the most widely ordered soups in Indian restaurants. Serving it topped with butter croutons makes this a comforting and filling meal by itself. Use fresh tomatoes for the best result. A drizzle of cashew cream on top is a wonderful addition.

---

2 tablespoons vegetable oil, divided

8 garlic cloves, coarsely chopped

1 inch ginger, peeled and chopped

8 tomatoes, coarsely chopped

¼ teaspoon ground cardamom or 1 cardamom pod

5 black peppercorns

1½ teaspoons salt, divided

2 teaspoons chili powder

½ teaspoon ground turmeric

2 cups vegetable broth or water

2 tablespoons vegan butter

½ cup finely chopped onion

½ cup fresh cilantro leaves and stems, coarsely chopped

Buttered croutons and freshly ground black pepper, for serving

---

1. In a pressure cooker, heat 1 tablespoon of oil. Add the garlic and ginger and fry.

2. Add the tomatoes, cardamom, peppercorns, 1 teaspoon of salt, chili powder, turmeric, and broth. Pressure cook for 3 whistles (about 20 minutes).

3. In a kadhai, heat the remaining 1 tablespoon of oil, followed by the butter. Add the onion and sauté until it turns translucent.

4. Add the tomato mixture and cilantro and cook for 5 minutes, stirring frequently.

5. Using a hand blender, puree the mixture.

6. Add the puree and return it to the kadhai. Add the remaining ½ teaspoon of salt. Cook over medium heat for another 15 minutes, stirring frequently.

7. Serve with buttered croutons and a grind of black pepper on top.

PER SERVING: Calories: 172; Total fat: 13g; Saturated fat: 2g; Sodium: 964mg; Carbohydrates: 15g; Sugar: 8g; Fiber: 4g; Protein: 3g

# Coriander Thambli
# (Cilantro Yogurt Soup)

**PREP TIME:** 5 minutes • **COOK TIME:** 10 minutes • **SERVES 4**

This delicious yogurt-based cold soup is from Udipi cuisine. It's a very easy and flavorful recipe that can be served not just as a soup but also as a side for rice.

½ cup plain unsweetened nondairy yogurt

2 teaspoons coconut oil, divided

1 teaspoon cumin seeds

2 green chile peppers, chopped

¾ cup chopped fresh cilantro

¼ cup unsweetened shredded coconut

¾ teaspoon salt

1 teaspoon mustard seeds

1 teaspoon urad dal

¼ teaspoon asafetida (hing)

1 dried red chile pepper

1. In a small bowl, whisk together the yogurt and 1 cup of water. Set aside.

2. In a small kadhai, heat 1 teaspoon of coconut oil. When it's hot, temper the cumin seeds. As they crackle, add the green chiles and cilantro. Sauté for 1 minute.

3. Take the kadhai off the heat and allow the mixture to cool.

4. In a food processor or mixer grinder, grind the mixture to a smooth paste with the coconut and ⅓ cup of water.

5. Add this ground paste to the whisked yogurt, along with the salt. Mix it all together.

6. Heat the remaining 1 teaspoon of coconut oil in a tadka pan. Temper the mustard seeds. Once they crackle, add the urad dal, asafetida, and dried chile. Fry until the lentils turn golden. Pour the tadka over the yogurt mix and serve immediately.

PER SERVING: Calories: 70; Total fat: 5g; Saturated fat: 3g; Sodium: 445mg; Carbohydrates: 6g; Sugar: 3g; Fiber: 1g; Protein: 2g

# Jeera Milagu Rasam
# (Cumin Pepper Rasam)

**PREP TIME:** 25 minutes, plus 20 minutes to soak • **COOK TIME:** 15 minutes • **SERVES 4**

Rasam is a lentil broth recipe from Tamil Nadu. This dish is served with rice and is the definition of comfort food. There are many varieties of rasam, and this is just one way of making it.

2 tablespoons tur dal

2 tablespoons jeera or cumin seeds

1 tablespoon black peppercorns

2 tomatoes, quartered

2 tablespoons tamarind paste

1 teaspoon ground turmeric

¾ teaspoon salt

¼ teaspoon asafetida (hing)

¼ cup finely chopped fresh cilantro

1 teaspoon vegetable oil

1 teaspoon mustard seeds

6 or 7 curry leaves

Steamed rice, for serving

1. Put the tur dal, jeera, and peppercorns in a bowl, add 1 cup of water, and soak for 20 minutes.

2. Transfer the mixture to a mixer grinder or food processor, add the tomatoes, and grind to a paste.

3. In a stockpot, combine 3 cups of water and the tamarind paste and stir well to dilute the paste.

4. Add the dal mixture, tamarind paste, turmeric, salt, and asafetida and mix everything well together.

5. Bring the mixture to a boil over low heat. Add the cilantro.

6. Heat the oil in a tadka pan, then temper the mustard seeds and curry leaves. Once the seeds crackle, pour this tadka over the boiling mixture.

7. Stir well until combined. Cook for 1 minute, then take it off the heat.

8. Serve hot with rice.

PER SERVING: Calories: 73; Total fat: 2g; Saturated fat: 0g; Sodium: 447mg; Carbohydrates: 12g; Sugar: 3g; Fiber: 3g; Protein: 3g

# Spicy Watermelon Soup

**PREP TIME:** 5 minutes • **COOK TIME:** 15 minutes • **SERVES 4**

Watermelon soup? Yes! Watermelon makes a comforting and refreshing soup to have on a dull day. A bit of freshly ground black pepper on top at the end adds a pungent note.

| | | |
|---|---|---|
| 2 pounds watermelon chunks | 1 tablespoon vegetable oil | 1 teaspoon red pepper flakes |
| ⅓ cup fresh mint leaves plus 3 or 4 for garnish | 1 tablespoon ginger-garlic paste | 2 teaspoons black salt |

1. In a food processor, puree the watermelon chunks with the mint leaves. You should get about 3½ cups of juice.

2. Heat the oil in a medium kadhai and fry the ginger-garlic paste and red pepper flakes for 1 minute.

3. Pour in the watermelon juice along with 1 cup of water. Cook over medium heat for 15 minutes.

4. Add the black salt and mix. The soup should have thickened. Take it off the heat.

5. Garnish with mint leaves and serve hot.

**INGREDIENT TIP:** Instead of the ginger-garlic paste, you can use freshly minced ginger and garlic. If you don't have black salt, use regular salt.

PER SERVING: Calories: 103; Total fat: 4g; Saturated fat: 1g; Sodium: 586mg; Carbohydrates: 18g; Sugar: 14g; Fiber: 1g; Protein: 2g

Biye Barir Pulao
(Bengali Vegetable
Pulao) page 73

# Rice

# White Basmati Rice

**PREP TIME:** 5 minutes • **COOK TIME:** 20 minutes • **SERVES 4**

Rice is one of the staple dishes in Indian cuisine. Be it plain white rice or flavored rice, an Indian meal is incomplete without it. Cooking white basmati rice is simple and forms the basis of many rice dishes. Look for good-quality organic basmati rice. Longer grains with a slight golden hue are preferred.

---

**1½ cups basmati rice**

**3 cups water or vegetable broth**

---

1. Rinse the rice a couple of times until the water runs clear. This washes away the excess starch and makes the rice less sticky. If you prefer the rice grains to be long and separate, soak the rice in water for 20 minutes, but this is optional. Drain the rice.

2. To cook in a rice cooker, transfer the rice to the rice cooker, add the water, and cook according to the instructions of the rice cooker. When done, open the cooker after 10 minutes. This prevents the rice being overly sticky or getting mushy.

3. To cook on the stovetop, transfer the rice to a pot, add the water, and bring to a boil, uncovered. Lower the heat, cover, and cook for 10 minutes or until the water has been absorbed fully and the rice is cooked. Take the pot off the heat. Let it sit for another 10 minutes and then open the lid.

4. Fluff with a fork. Serve hot.

**PREP TIP:** You can also cook rice in an Instant Pot. Cook it in rice or manual mode for 4 minutes and release the pressure immediately.

PER SERVING: Calories: 263; Total fat: 0g; Saturated fat: 0g; Sodium: 1mg; Carbohydrates: 58g; Sugar: 0g; Fiber: 1g; Protein: 5g

# Jeera Garlic Rice

**PREP TIME:** 5 minutes, plus 20 minutes to soak • **COOK TIME:** 15 minutes • **SERVES 4**

Garlic-flavored jeera rice is made with basmati rice and cumin seeds. It's an aromatic Indian side dish that's served in every Indian restaurant and on happy occasions. This classic, mildly spiced recipe for jeera rice is delicious, quick, and easy to make. For a more authentic flavor, look for shah jeera instead of cumin. To save prep time, skip soaking the rice and cook with an extra ½ cup of water.

2 cups basmati rice

2 tablespoons vegetable oil

2 bay leaves

2-inch cinnamon stick

1 tablespoon cashews

5 black peppercorns

5 cloves

1 cardamom pod

6 garlic cloves, minced

2 green chile peppers

4 tablespoons chopped fresh cilantro, divided

2 teaspoons salt

1. Rinse the rice a couple of times until the water runs clear. Soak the rice in water for 20 minutes, then drain.

2. Heat the oil in a medium kadhai over medium heat. Fry the bay leaves, cinnamon, cashews, peppercorns, cloves, and cardamom for about 30 seconds.

3. Add the garlic, green chiles, and 2 tablespoons of cilantro. Fry until the garlic turns light golden.

4. Add the rice. Toast for 1 minute without stirring.

5. Add 3½ cups of water and the salt. Stir, cover, and cook for 10 minutes.

6. When the rice is cooked, garnish with the remaining 2 tablespoons of cilantro. Mix well and take the kadhai off the heat.

VARIATION TIP: Add more veggies like green beans, carrots, green peas, or even potatoes to make the rice more flavorful and nourishing. You can also make this in the Instant Pot. Follow all the steps and cook it in manual mode for 4 minutes. Release pressure naturally.

PER SERVING: Calories: 443; Total fat: 9g; Saturated fat: 1g; Sodium: 1167mg; Carbohydrates: 82g; Sugar: 1g; Fiber: 2g; Protein: 8g

# Matar Pulao (Green Pea Pilaf)

**PREP TIME:** 15 minutes • **COOK TIME:** 15 minutes • **SERVES 4**

This simple but great-tasting recipe is an aromatic dish made with peas, rice, and spices. This is another restaurant favorite that can easily be re-created at home, especially if you have leftover rice.

---

3 tablespoons vegan butter or vegetable oil

1 onion, finely chopped, divided

6 garlic cloves, minced

½ inch ginger, grated

6 cashews

2 green chile peppers

⅓ cup unsweetened shredded coconut

1 teaspoon mustard seeds

1 teaspoon cumin seeds

4 tablespoons chopped fresh cilantro, divided

1 teaspoon ground turmeric

1 teaspoon ground cumin

1 cup green peas

1½ cups basmati rice, cooked (see page 66)

1½ teaspoons salt

1 teaspoon garam masala

---

1. Heat 1 tablespoon of butter in a pan over medium heat and fry half the onion until translucent.

2. Add the garlic, ginger, cashews, green chiles, and coconut. Fry for 3 minutes, then take the pan off the heat.

3. Allow the mixture to cool, then transfer it to a mixer grinder, add 2 tablespoons of water, and grind it to a smooth paste.

4. Heat the remaining 2 tablespoons of butter in a tadka pan. Temper the mustard seeds and cumin seeds. Once they crackle, add 2 tablespoons of cilantro and the remaining onion. Sauté until the onion turns translucent.

5. Add the ground paste. Mix and sauté for 3 minutes over medium heat until the oil separates. Stir in the turmeric and ground cumin. Fry for 3 minutes.

6. Add the green peas, mix, and cook for 2 minutes. Add the cooked rice and salt. Mix well and cook for 1 minute.

7. Add the garam masala and remaining 2 tablespoons of cilantro. Mix everything well and serve.

PER SERVING: Calories: 289; Total fat: 15g; Saturated fat: 3g; Sodium: 882mg; Carbohydrates: 34g; Sugar: 5g; Fiber: 4g; Protein: 6g

# Cilantro Pot Rice

**PREP TIME:** 15 minutes • **COOK TIME:** 5 minutes • **SERVES 4**

Normally used for garnish, aromatic cilantro fried in oil imparts a truly unique flavor to this fried rice, which is great with Restaurant-Style Tomato Soup (page 60) and Chatpata Aloo Salad (page 19).

| | | |
|---|---|---|
| 1 tablespoon vegan butter or vegetable oil | 1 tablespoon red pepper flakes | 1 bell pepper (any color), chopped |
| 1 teaspoon cumin seeds | 1 cup chopped fresh cilantro | 1½ cups basmati rice, cooked (see page 66) |
| 9 garlic cloves | ½ cup green peas | 1½ teaspoons salt |

1. Heat the butter in a medium kadhai over medium heat and temper the cumin seeds.

2. Once the seeds crackle, add the garlic, red pepper flakes, and cilantro. Fry for 1 minute.

3. Add the green peas and bell pepper. Mix and sauté for 2 minutes.

4. Add the cooked rice and salt. Give it all a good mix and cook for 1 minute.

**VARIATION TIP:** Add 1 teaspoon ajinomoto or MSG along with the salt for a different flavor. You can also use other greens, such as spinach, instead of the cilantro.

PER SERVING: Calories: 157; Total fat: 4g; Saturated fat: 1g; Sodium: 878mg; Carbohydrates: 27g; Sugar: 2g; Fiber: 2g; Protein: 4g

# Aloo Ki Tahari
# (Potato Pulao)

**PREP TIME:** 10 minutes, plus 20 minutes to soak • **COOK TIME:** 30 minutes • **SERVES 4**

This one-pot rice recipe from Awadhi cuisine is mildly flavored and aromatic. Potatoes and rice cooked together in spices make an extremely delicious pulao.

---

2 cups basmati rice

2 tablespoons vegan butter or ghee

1 tablespoon vegetable oil

1 teaspoon cumin seeds

1 cinnamon stick

5 cloves

1 cardamom pod or ¼ teaspoon ground cardamom

3 green chile peppers, slit

7 garlic cloves, minced

1 cup sliced onion

3 potatoes, peeled and cut into wedges

1½ teaspoons salt, divided

2 tomatoes, finely chopped

¼ cup plus 2 tablespoons chopped fresh cilantro

1 teaspoon chili powder

1 teaspoon ground turmeric

1 teaspoon garam masala or biryani masala

½ teaspoon rose water (optional)

---

1. Rinse the rice a couple of times until the water runs clear. Soak the rice in water for 20 minutes, then drain.

2. Heat the butter and oil in a large pan over medium heat. Temper the cumin seeds. Once they crackle, add the cinnamon, cloves, and cardamom. Sauté for 15 seconds.

3. Add the green chiles, garlic, and onion and sauté for 2 minutes.

4. Add the potatoes and 1 teaspoon of salt. Sauté for 5 minutes or until the potatoes are almost cooked.

5. Add the tomatoes, ¼ cup of cilantro, and ⅓ cup of water. Cover and cook for 5 minutes.

6. Add the chili powder, turmeric, garam masala, and remaining ½ teaspoon of salt and fry for 20 seconds.

7. Add the rice and 3 cups of water. Mix, cover, and cook for 10 minutes or until the rice is done.

8. Sprinkle with the rose water (if using) and fluff the rice with a fork.

PREP TIP: Cut up the potatoes ahead of time and soak them in water to prevent them from blackening, then drain just before using.

VARIATION TIP: You can prepare this recipe using leftover rice. You can also add more veggies, such as carrots, beans, and green peas, to make it more substantial.

PER SERVING: Calories: 617; Total fat: 12g; Saturated fat: 1g; Sodium: 911mg; Carbohydrates: 116g; Sugar: 6g; Fiber: 7g; Protein: 12g

# Bell Pepper Rice

**PREP TIME:** 15 minutes • **COOK TIME:** 5 minutes • **SERVES 6**

Packed with flavor, this fried rice recipe is quick and easy to make. Use leftover rice or cook some ahead and let it cool before beginning this recipe. Serve with Kachumber (page 18).

1 tablespoon vegetable oil

1 teaspoon cumin seeds

6 curry leaves

2 green chile peppers

1 tablespoon ginger-garlic paste

1 cup chopped onion

1 bell pepper (any color), chopped

½ cup green peas

2 tablespoons sambhar powder

1 teaspoon ground turmeric

1 teaspoon chili powder

1 teaspoon ground coriander

1 teaspoon ground cumin

1½ cups basmati rice, cooked (see page 66) and cooled

1½ teaspoons salt

⅓ cup chopped fresh cilantro

1. Heat the oil in a pan over medium heat and temper the cumin seeds.

2. Once they begin to crackle, add the curry leaves, green chiles, ginger-garlic paste, and onion. Sauté until the onion turns translucent. Add the bell pepper and green peas and sauté for 3 minutes. Add the sambhar powder, turmeric, chili powder, coriander, and ground cumin and sauté for 1 minute.

3. Add the cooked rice and salt. Mix everything together well.

4. Garnish with the cilantro.

**VARIATION TIP:** Use a mix of different bell peppers to give the dish a pop of color.

PER SERVING: Calories: 120; Total fat: 3g; Saturated fat: 0g; Sodium: 600mg; Carbohydrates: 21g; Sugar: 4g; Fiber: 2g; Protein: 3g

# Biye Barir Pulao
# (Bengali Vegetable Pulao)

**PREP TIME:** 10 minutes, plus 20 minutes to soak • **COOK TIME:** 20 minutes • **SERVES 4**

This is a Bengali-style pulao rice that's aromatic because of the spices used and wholesome because of the veggies and basmati rice. This dish is served in Bengal oil on almost all happy occasions.

1½ teaspoons salt

1 teaspoon garam masala

1 teaspoon freshly ground black pepper

1 tablespoon vegetable oil or vegan ghee

1 cinnamon stick

4 cloves

2 bay leaves

1 cardamom pod

2 tablespoons cashews

2 green chile peppers, halved

⅓ cup peeled and chopped carrots

⅓ cup green peas

½ cup chopped green beans

2 tablespoons raisins

1½ cups basmati rice, cooked (see page 66)

1. Mix the salt, garam masala, and black pepper in a small bowl and set aside.

2. Heat the oil in a medium kadhai over medium heat. Sauté the cinnamon, cloves, bay leaves, cardamom, and cashews for 1 minute. Add the green chiles and fry for 30 seconds. Add the carrots, green peas, green beans, and raisins. Sauté over high heat until they are cooked.

3. Turn off the heat and spoon half the cooked rice over the veggies. Sprinkle with half of the prepared spice mix and then add the remaining rice. Sprinkle with the remaining spice mix.

4. Using two spoons, lightly toss the rice so that everything gets mixed without mashing the rice.

5. Cover the pot and cook over medium heat for another 6 minutes. Keep stirring to ensure that the rice doesn't stick to the bottom of the kadhai.

PER SERVING: Calories: 362; Total fat: 6g; Saturated fat: 1g; Sodium: 884mg; Carbohydrates: 69g; Sugar: 6g; Fiber: 3g; Protein: 7g

# Soya Biryani

**PREP TIME:** 15 minutes, plus 30 minutes to soak and 20 minutes to marinate
**COOK TIME:** 30 minutes • **SERVES 4**

If you're looking for something vegan with the same texture and flavor as chicken, then textured vegetable protein (TVP) is a very good option. It's rich in protein and it absorbs the flavors of the dish. When cooked with rice, it elevates the flavor of this aromatic biryani to new heights. Serve with Kachumber (page 18), Tomato Saar (page 44), or even Mushroom Potato Vindaloo (page 97).

1 cup rice

2½ teaspoons salt, divided

1 teaspoon ground turmeric, divided

1 cup soya chunks (TVP)

3 tablespoons plain unsweetened nondairy yogurt

1 teaspoon chili powder

2 tablespoons vegetable oil

1 bay leaf

5 cloves

4 black peppercorns

1 cardamom pod

1 tablespoon ginger-garlic paste

1 cup chopped onion

2 green chile peppers, chopped

2 tomatoes, chopped

1 teaspoon chili powder

1 teaspoon garam masala

2 tablespoons chopped fresh mint leaves

⅓ cup plus 2 tablespoons chopped fresh cilantro

1. Rinse the rice a couple of times until the water runs clear. Soak the rice in water for 30 minutes, then drain.

2. Pour 2 cups of water into a pot, add 1 teaspoon of salt and ½ teaspoon of turmeric, and bring to a boil.

3. Add the soya chunks and cook for 15 minutes. Take the pot off the heat and allow it to cool.

4. Squeeze out the water from the soya chunks and transfer them to a bowl.

5. Add the yogurt, chili powder, ½ teaspoon of salt, and the remaining ½ teaspoon of turmeric. Stir well to coat the soya chunks. Let marinate for 20 minutes.

6. Heat the oil in a large kadhai over medium heat. Fry the bay leaf, cloves, peppercorns, and cardamom for 30 seconds. Add the ginger-garlic paste, onion, and green chiles. Sauté until the onion turns translucent.

7. Add the tomatoes and cook until they turn soft and pulpy. Add the chili powder, garam masala, mint, and ⅓ cup of cilantro. Sauté for 1 minute.

8. Add the marinated soya chunks along with the remaining 1 teaspoon of salt. Mix and cook for 1 minute.

9. Add the rinsed rice and 1½ cups of water. Mix, cover, and cook for 10 minutes.

10. Add the remaining 2 tablespoons of cilantro and mix well.

VARIATION TIP: Swap the soya chunks for chickpeas to make chickpea biryani.

PER SERVING: Calories: 331; Total fat: 11g; Saturated fat: 2g; Sodium: 932mg; Carbohydrates: 50g; Sugar: 5g; Fiber: 4g; Protein: 11g

# Cabbage Fried Rice

**PREP TIME:** 15 minutes • **COOK TIME:** 15 minutes • **SERVES 4**

Indo-Chinese cuisine combines elements from both Indian and Chinese cuisines, but it's very distinct from either. This recipe is an Indo-Chinese fried rice with cabbage as the main ingredient. It is very flavorful and quick to make. It's also a great way to make use of leftover rice.

| | | |
|---|---|---|
| 2 tablespoons vegetable oil | 3 green chile peppers, minced | 1 teaspoon ground cumin |
| 1 teaspoon fennel seeds | 1 cup chopped onion | 1 teaspoon freshly ground black pepper |
| 1 tablespoon urad dal | ½ cup green peas | 1½ cups basmati rice |
| 1 tablespoon chana dal | 8 ounces cabbage, shredded | 2 teaspoons soy sauce or coconut aminos |
| 10 garlic cloves, sliced | 2 teaspoons salt | |
| 1 inch ginger, minced | | |

1. Heat the oil in a pan over medium heat. Temper the fennel seeds. Once they crackle, add the urad dal and chana dal. Sauté until the dal turns light golden.

2. Add the garlic, ginger, and green chiles. When the garlic turns golden, add the onion and sauté until translucent.

3. Add the green peas and cabbage. Mix, cover, and cook for 5 minutes, stirring occasionally.

4. Once the cabbage is cooked, add the salt, cumin, and black pepper.

5. Add the cooked rice and soy sauce. Mix everything together lightly and serve.

VARIATION TIP: Instead of shredding your own cabbage, you can use the preshredded cabbage that comes in bags for coleslaw. Instead of fennel seeds, you can use cumin seeds or skip them.

PER SERVING: Calories: 400; Total fat: 8g; Saturated fat: 1g; Sodium: 1162mg; Carbohydrates: 74g; Sugar: 6g; Fiber: 5g; Protein: 9g

# Tamarind Mustard Chitranna Rice

**PREP TIME:** 15 minutes • **COOK TIME:** 15 minutes • **SERVES 4**

There are many varieties of this South Indian–style rice preparation, which is seasoned with tamarind and mustard and called chitranna. Spice works really well in this recipe, but you can reduce the chiles if you don't want it quite so spicy.

¼ cup chana dal

6 dried red chile peppers

¼ teaspoon fenugreek seeds

10 curry leaves

2 teaspoons mustard powder

¼ cup vegetable oil

2 teaspoons mustard seeds

2 tablespoons urad dal

½ teaspoon asafetida (hing)

2 green chile peppers, chopped

2 dried red chile peppers

¼ cup roasted peanuts

1 teaspoon ground turmeric

2 tablespoons tamarind paste

2 cups basmati rice, cooked (see page 66)

1½ teaspoons salt

1. In a pan, dry-roast the chana dal, dried red chiles, fenugreek, and curry leaves over medium heat for 3 minutes or until the lentils are golden.

2. Remove the pan from the heat and allow the contents to cool. Transfer to a food processor or mixer grinder, add the mustard powder, and grind to a powder. Set aside.

3. In the same pan, heat the oil over medium heat. Temper the mustard seeds. Once they crackle, add the urad dal and asafetida. Fry until the lentils turn golden.

4. Add the green chiles and red chile peppers and fry for 1 minute.

5. Add the peanuts and fry for another 30 seconds, then add the turmeric and ground spice mix. Fry for 1 more minute.

6. Add the tamarind paste and cook for 30 seconds.

7. Add the cooked rice and salt. Mix together so the spices coat the rice.

PER SERVING: Calories: 553; Total fat: 19g; Saturated fat: 3g; Sodium: 907mg; Carbohydrates: 85g; Sugar: 3g; Fiber: 3g; Protein: 10g

# Lentil Pilaf

**PREP TIME:** 10 minutes, plus 2 hours to soak • **COOK TIME:** 20 minutes • **SERVES 4**

This nutritious, tasty pilaf is similar to mujaddara, a classic Arabic dish, and is perfect for weeknight dinners. Serve with Tomato Saar (page 44), any curry you like, and a salad.

---

½ cup lentils (masoor dal, red, brown, or green)

1½ cups basmati rice

2 tablespoons vegetable oil

2 bay leaves

1 cinnamon stick

5 cloves

1 teaspoon cumin seeds

2 green chile peppers, minced

1 tablespoon ginger paste

1 tablespoon garlic paste

1 cup chopped onion

1 cup mixed chopped veggies (such as green beans, carrots, green peas)

2 teaspoons salt

1 teaspoon chili powder

½ teaspoon ground turmeric

¼ cup chopped fresh cilantro

---

1. Rinse the lentils, soak them in water for 2 hours, then drain. At the same time, rinse the rice a couple of times until the water runs clear. Soak the rice in water for 20 minutes, then drain.

2. Heat the oil in a pan over medium heat. Fry the bay leaves, cinnamon, cloves, and cumin. Once the seeds begin to crackle, add the green chile peppers, ginger paste, and garlic paste and fry for 1 minute.

3. Add the onion and sauté until translucent, then add the mixed veggies and continue to sauté for 2 minutes. Stir in the soaked lentils and cook for another 2 minutes.

4. Add the salt, chili powder, turmeric, and soaked rice and stir.

5. Add 3 cups of water, mix, and cover the pan. Cook for 9 minutes or until the rice is cooked.

6. Stir in the cilantro and serve.

PER SERVING: Calories: 463; Total fat: 8g; Saturated fat: 1g; Sodium: 1102mg; Carbohydrates: 84g; Sugar: 4g; Fiber: 7g; Protein: 15g

# Mixed Sprout Fried Rice

**PREP TIME:** 10 minutes, plus 30 minutes to soak • **COOK TIME:** 20 minutes • **SERVES 4**

This flavorful dish is made with a variety of sprouts that bring crunch, nutrition, and flavor to make an appetizing weeknight meal. It's a great way to incorporate protein with rice.

1½ cups basmati rice

1 tablespoon vegetable oil

1 tablespoon sugar

1 teaspoon cumin seeds

1 bay leaf

4 cloves

1 cardamom pod

1-inch cinnamon stick

5 black peppercorns

1 tablespoon ginger-garlic paste

2 green chile peppers

⅓ cup chopped fresh cilantro

1 cup mixed sprouts

2 cups chopped spinach

1 teaspoon ground cumin

1 teaspoon ground coriander

1 teaspoon chili powder

1 teaspoon black salt

1 teaspoon salt

Raita, for serving

1. Rinse the rice a couple of times until the water runs clear. Soak the rice in water for 30 minutes, then drain.

2. Heat the oil in a medium kadhai over medium heat. When the oil is hot, add the sugar, but do not stir it until it begins to melt.

3. Add the cumin seeds, bay leaf, cloves, cardamom, cinnamon, and peppercorns. Sauté for 30 seconds.

4. Add the ginger-garlic paste, green chile peppers, and cilantro. Fry for 1 minute, then add the rice and sauté for another minute.

5. Stir in the mixed sprouts, spinach, ground cumin, coriander, chili powder, black salt, and salt. Cook for 2 minutes, then add 4 cups of water, stir, cover the pan, and cook for 10 minutes. Serve with raita.

**VARIATION TIP:** Instead of mixed sprouts, you can also use one variety of sprouts, such as moong beans, moth beans, or chana sprouts. Instead of spinach, swap in fenugreek leaves for a lovely aromatic flavor.

PER SERVING: Calories: 347; Total fat: 4g; Saturated fat: 0g; Sodium: 852mg; Carbohydrates: 69g; Sugar: 4g; Fiber: 2g; Protein: 8g

# Broccoli Masala Khichdi
# (Broccoli with Lentils and Rice Mash)

**PREP TIME:** 15 minutes, plus 30 minutes to soak • **COOK TIME:** 45 minutes • **SERVES 6**

Khichdi is the ultimate comfort food for Indians. Rice and lentils are cooked together and tempered with mild spices. Broccoli is the surprise ingredient in this simple and humble dish. It is healthy and so easy on the stomach that it's safe for toddlers and those recovering from sickness. You can add any vegetables you have on hand to bump up the nutrition. Unlike many other rice recipes, the texture of this dish is best when made with freshly made rice rather than leftover rice. If you don't have all the dals, no problem; just use the same amount of one type. Serve this khichdi with papad and pickle.

½ cup tur dal

¼ cup chana dal

¼ cup masoor dal

3½ teaspoons vegan butter or vegetable oil

3 teaspoons cumin seeds, divided

1½ teaspoons ginger paste

2 teaspoons ground turmeric, divided

2 teaspoons salt, divided

1 tablespoon ginger paste

4 dried red chile peppers, divided

6 curry leaves

6 garlic cloves, minced

2 green chile peppers, minced

½ cup chopped onion

2 tomatoes, chopped

2 teaspoons chili powder, divided

1 teaspoon amchur powder

1 teaspoon ground coriander

2 cups broccoli florets

1 cup basmati rice, cooked (see page 66)

1 teaspoon kasuri methi (optional)

1 teaspoon garam masala

¼ cup chopped fresh cilantro

¼ teaspoon asafetida (hing)

1 tablespoon fried onions

1. Rinse and soak the tur dal, chana dal, and masoor dal for 30 minutes. Drain and set aside.

2. Heat 1½ teaspoons of butter in a pressure cooker. Once it melts, temper 1 teaspoon of cumin seeds and the ginger paste. Fry for 30 seconds, then add the drained lentils and sauté for 1 minute.

3. Add 3 cups of water, 1 teaspoon of turmeric, and 1 teaspoon of salt. Mix and pressure cook the lentils for 3 whistles (about 20 minutes). Let the pressure release naturally.

4. Add 1 cup of water and mix and mash the lentils.

5. Melt 1 teaspoon of butter in a pan over medium heat. Temper 1 teaspoon of cumin seeds. Add 2 dried red chiles, the curry leaves, garlic, and green chiles and fry for 30 seconds.

6. Add the onion and cook until translucent, then stir in the tomatoes and remaining 1 teaspoon of salt. Cook until the tomatoes turn soft and pulpy.

7. Add the remaining 1 teaspoon of turmeric, 1 teaspoon of chili powder, and the amchur and coriander. Fry for a minute, then add the broccoli and ½ cup of water. Mix, cover, and cook for 6 minutes.

8. Stir in the mashed lentils and then the cooked rice. Cover the pan and cook for 3 minutes.

9. Garnish with the kasuri methi (if using), garam masala, and cilantro.

10. The final step is to prepare the tadka. Heat the remaining 1 teaspoon of butter in a tadka pan. Temper the remaining 1 teaspoon of cumin seeds. Once they crackle, add the remaining 2 dried red chiles, remaining 1 teaspoon of chili powder, the asafetida, and the fried onions. Fry for 20 seconds, then pour the tadka over the khichdi.

VARIATION TIP: Add more veggies like potatoes, cauliflower, carrots, and green peas for extra nutrition.

PER SERVING: Calories: 289; Total fat: 2g; Saturated fat: 0g; Sodium: 823mg; Carbohydrates: 56g; Sugar: 6g; Fiber: 11g; Protein: 12g

# Thayir Sadam
# (Tempered Yogurt Rice)

**PREP TIME:** 15 minutes • **COOK TIME:** 5 minutes • **SERVES 6**

More popularly known as curd rice, this traditional rice recipe from the south of India is mixed with yogurt and tempered with spices to make it flavorful. It is very good for digestion and is usually eaten at the end of the meal. If you like, add some grated carrots and pomegranate seeds to add color and extra nutrition. Serve chilled with some pickle.

3 cups cooked basmati rice (see page 66)

1⅓ cups plain unsweetened nondairy yogurt

1 teaspoon salt

⅓ cup chopped fresh cilantro

1 teaspoon vegetable oil

2 teaspoons mustard seeds

2 teaspoons urad dal

¼ teaspoon asafetida (hing)

2 green chile peppers, minced

8 curry leaves

1. In a large bowl, combine the rice, yogurt, salt, and cilantro.

2. Heat the oil in a tadka pan over medium heat. Temper the mustard seeds, and once they begin to splutter, add the urad dal, asafetida, green chile peppers, and curry leaves.

3. Fry until the lentils turn golden. Pour this tadka over the curd rice and stir it in.

**PREP TIP:** If the curd rice gets too thick, add ½ cup water or some diluted yogurt. Adjust the salt accordingly.

**VARIATION TIP:** If you like, add some grated carrots and pomegranate seeds to add color and extra nutrition.

PER SERVING: Calories: 152; Total fat: 3g; Saturated fat: 1g; Sodium: 415mg; Carbohydrates: 26g; Sugar: 3g; Fiber: 1g; Protein: 5g

# Meethe Chawal (Sweet Rice)

**PREP TIME:** 5 minutes, plus 30 minutes to soak • **COOK TIME:** 15 minutes • **SERVES 4**

Also known as zarda pulao, this sweet dish is perfect for any gathering and is wonderful served with ice cream. A teaspoon of rose water or kewra stirred in at the end gives an enticing aroma.

1½ cups basmati rice

½ teaspoon saffron strands

Pinch salt

3 cardamom pods, divided

3 tablespoons coconut oil

1 cinnamon stick

4 cloves

2 tablespoons cashews

1 tablespoon chopped almonds

1 tablespoon raisins

¼ cup unsweetened shredded coconut

1¼ cups sugar

Pinch ground nutmeg (optional)

1. Rinse the rice a couple of times until the water runs clear. Soak the rice in water for 30 minutes, then drain. Soak the saffron in 3 tablespoons of water for 15 minutes.

2. In a pot, combine 4 cups of water, the salt, and 2 cardamom pods. Bring to a boil, then add the soaked rice. Cover the pot and cook for 7 minutes or until the rice is almost done.

3. Drain the rice, then transfer it to a bowl and set aside.

4. In the same pot, heat the oil over medium heat. Fry the cinnamon, cloves, remaining cardamom pod, cashews, almonds, and raisins for 30 seconds.

5. Add the cooked rice and mix lightly to avoid breaking the grains. Add the saffron with its soaking water and stir to coat the rice. Keep sautéing until the rice absorbs some color from the saffron.

6. Stir in the coconut, then add the sugar. Do not stir. Cover and cook for 2 minutes.

7. When the sugar melts, open the lid and sauté until all the moisture evaporates. Stir in the nutmeg (if using). Serve hot or cold.

PER SERVING: Calories: 686; Total fat: 16g; Saturated fat: 11g; Sodium: 43mg; Carbohydrates: 132g; Sugar: 70g; Fiber: 2g; Protein: 7g

# Vangi Bhath (Eggplant Rice)

**PREP TIME:** 25 minutes • **COOK TIME:** 20 minutes • **SERVES 6**

Even if you are not a big fan of eggplant, give this dish a try. You may just become a convert. The special masala used here gives the rice an aromatic flavor. To save prep time, prepare the masala in advance and keep it in an airtight container until needed. You can also cook the rice ahead of time or store in the refrigerator. Serve with Kachumber (page 18) or raita.

2½ cups cubed eggplant

3 teaspoons salt, divided

2 tablespoons chana dal, divided

2 teaspoons urad dal, divided

4 dried red chile peppers

10 cloves

5 black peppercorns

1 cinnamon stick

½ teaspoon cumin seeds

6 fenugreek seeds (optional)

2 tablespoons peanuts

½ teaspoon poppy seeds (optional)

¼ cup unsweetened shredded coconut

2 tablespoons vegetable oil

1 teaspoon mustard seeds

6 curry leaves

¼ teaspoon asafetida (hing)

1 cup sliced onion

½ teaspoon ground turmeric

2 tablespoons tamarind paste

¼ cup water or vegetable broth

2 cups basmati rice, cooked (see page 66)

3 tablespoons chopped fresh cilantro

1. Put the eggplant in a medium bowl, add 1 teaspoon of salt, and cover with water. Set aside to soak.

2. In a large kadhai over medium heat, dry-roast 1 tablespoon of chana dal, 1 teaspoon of urad dal, the dried red chiles, cloves, peppercorns, cinnamon, cumin, fenugreek, peanuts, and poppy seeds (if using) for 1 minute or until the lentils turn golden.

3. Add the coconut and dry-roast for 40 seconds. Transfer the mixture to a plate and allow it to cool.

4. In a food processor or mixer grinder, process the mixture to a smooth powder and set aside.

5. In the same kadhai, heat the oil. Temper the mustard seeds. Once they crackle, add the remaining 1 tablespoon of chana dal, remaining 1 teaspoon of urad dal, the curry leaves, and the asafetida.

6. Sauté until the lentils turn golden, then add the sliced onion and sauté until translucent.

7. Drain the eggplant and stir it in, along with the turmeric. Cook for 2 minutes. Add the tamarind paste. Mix, cover, and cook for 4 minutes.

8. Pour in the water and remaining 2 teaspoons of salt. Cover and cook for 4 more minutes or until the eggplant is cooked.

9. Add the cooked rice along with the ground masala and mix well. Stir in the cilantro and serve.

PREP TIP: Soaking the eggplant in salt water prevents it from discoloring.

VARIATION TIP: Add potatoes along with the eggplant. They make a great combo. You can also serve the stir-fried eggplant as a side without adding the rice.

PER SERVING: Calories: 331; Total fat: 8g; Saturated fat: 2g; Sodium: 489mg; Carbohydrates: 58g; Sugar: 4g; Fiber: 3g; Protein: 6g

# Peanut Rice

**PREP TIME:** 15 minutes • **COOK TIME:** 10 minutes • **SERVES 4**

This is one of those recipes that comes together quickly if you have the spice mix ready. Make it ahead and keep it in an airtight container so you can whip up this dish whenever you want. Ground peanuts, spices, and lentils give this rice dish a unique nutty flavor.

4 teaspoons vegetable oil, divided

½ cup peanuts

2 tablespoons chana dal

1 tablespoon urad dal

1 tablespoon black or white sesame seeds

1 teaspoon cumin seeds

8 curry leaves

6 dried red chile peppers

1 teaspoon mustard seeds

2 cups basmati rice, cooked (see page 66)

2 teaspoons salt

¼ cup chopped fresh cilantro

1. In a medium kadhai, heat 1 teaspoon of oil on medium heat. Add the peanuts, chana dal, urad dal, sesame seeds, cumin, curry leaves, and dried red peppers. Roast for 3 minutes, then transfer to a plate to cool. Transfer to a food processor or mixer grinder and process to a fine powder.

2. In the same kadhai, heat the remaining 3 teaspoons of oil. When the oil is hot, temper the mustard seeds. When the seeds crackle, add the peanut powder, followed by the cooked rice and salt. Mix well and cook for 5 minutes. Stir in the cilantro and serve.

PREP TIP: After roasting the spices, don't leave them in the hot pan. Transfer them to a plate to prevent them from burning.

PER SERVING: Calories: 514; Total fat: 16g; Saturated fat: 2g; Sodium: 1071mg; Carbohydrates: 81g; Sugar: 1g; Fiber: 4g; Protein: 12g

Cauliflower
Tikka Masala
page 92

CHAPTER 5

# Curries and Stir-Fries

# Amritsari Soya Curry

**PREP TIME:** 15 minutes • **COOK TIME:** 10 minutes • **SERVES 4**

Amritsari food is known for its spicy, tangy flavors. It's also known for its meat-based curries. Using soya chunks is a perfect substitute for meat without compromising on the texture or flavor. The tea bag in this recipe is used to provide dark color, not taste, so skip it if you don't have it, and don't be tempted to use loose tea instead. Serve with any flatbread or rice.

---

1 cinnamon stick

4 bay leaves, divided

10 black peppercorns

6 cloves

2 cardamom pods

1 Indian tea bag (optional)

¼ teaspoon baking soda

2 teaspoons salt, divided

1½ cups soya chunks, regular or mini

1 tablespoon cumin seeds

1 tablespoon coriander seeds

1 teaspoon fennel seeds

4 dried red chile peppers

1 tablespoon kasuri methi (optional)

1 teaspoon chili powder

1 teaspoon garam masala

1 teaspoon amchur powder (optional)

½ teaspoon ground turmeric

¼ teaspoon asafetida (hing)

2 tablespoons vegetable oil

1 cinnamon stick

1 cup peeled and cubed potatoes

1 tablespoon ginger paste

1 tablespoon garlic paste

2 tomatoes, pureed

1 cup fried onions

1 green chile pepper, halved

¼ cup chopped fresh cilantro

---

1. In a pressure cooker over medium heat, combine 4 cups of water, the cinnamon, 2 bay leaves, the peppercorns, the cloves, the cardamon, the tea bag (if using), the baking soda, 1 teaspoon of salt, and the soya chunks.

2. Close the lid and cook for 1 whistle (about 15 minutes).

3. Release the pressure naturally and then open the lid. Drain and reserve the water for the gravy. Discard the whole spices and tea bag. Press the soya chunks with a ladle to squeeze out excess water. Set aside.

4. In a pan over medium heat, dry-roast the cumin seeds, coriander seeds, fennel seeds, dried red peppers, and kasuri methi (if using) for 3 minutes or until the spices become darker. Be careful to not burn them.

5. Transfer to a bowl and allow the spices to cool. Then transfer the contents to a food processor or mixer grinder and process to a powder. Return the powder to the bowl and add the chili powder, garam masala, amchur powder (if using), turmeric, and asafetida. Mix and set aside.

6. Heat the oil in a medium kadhai over medium heat. Add the cinnamon stick and remaining 2 bay leaves and fry for 30 seconds.

7. Add the potatoes and sauté for 5 minutes, tossing them frequently so they cook evenly.

8. Stir in the ginger paste and garlic paste. Fry for another 30 seconds, then add the tomato puree and remaining 1 teaspoon of salt. Mix and bring to a boil.

9. Add the spice powder and half of the reserved cooking water. Mix, cover, and cook for 3 minutes.

10. Add the soya chunks and remaining reserved cooking water. Stir in the fried onions, cover, and cook for 5 minutes.

11. Stir in the green chile pepper and cilantro and serve.

VARIATION TIP: Replace the amchur powder with 1½ teaspoons of tamarind paste. Instead of fried onions, you can use fresh onions. If doing so, add them before the potatoes, and fry them.

PER SERVING: Calories: 239; Total fat: 15g; Saturated fat: 2g; Sodium: 1019mg; Carbohydrates: 21g; Sugar: 5g; Fiber: 5g; Protein: 11g

# Cauliflower Tikka Masala

**PREP TIME:** 15 minutes • **COOK TIME:** 30 minutes • **SERVES 4**

This recipe is a vegan take on the always popular chicken tikka masala and uses cauliflower instead of chicken. Using red, yellow, or orange bell pepper rather than green gives the dish the desired color. Serve this lovely recipe with flatbread or rice to soak up the deliciously rich and creamy sauce.

1½ teaspoons vegetable oil

1 teaspoon mustard seeds

1 teaspoon cumin seeds

1 tablespoon ginger paste

1 tablespoon garlic paste

2 green chile peppers

1 cup coarsely chopped onion

3 tomatoes, coarsely chopped

½ bell pepper (any color), coarsely chopped

⅓ cup plus ¼ cup chopped fresh cilantro

1½ cups full-fat coconut milk, divided

2½ teaspoons salt, divided

1 teaspoon ground turmeric

1 head cauliflower, cut into florets

1 teaspoon chili powder

1 teaspoon ground coriander

1 teaspoon ground cumin

1 teaspoon garam masala

1 teaspoon kasuri methi (optional)

1. In a pan over medium heat, heat the oil. Temper the mustard and cumin seeds. When they crackle, add the ginger paste, garlic paste, and green chile peppers. Sauté for 30 seconds.

2. Add the onion and sauté until translucent. Add the tomatoes, bell pepper, and ⅓ cup of cilantro. Sauté for 5 minutes, then take the pan off the heat and allow to cool.

3. When cool, transfer the ingredients to a food processor, add ½ cup of coconut milk, and process to a smooth paste. You can strain this sauce if you want.

4. Fill a large pot with water, add 1 teaspoon of salt and the turmeric, and bring to a boil over medium heat. Add the cauliflower and boil for 10 minutes. Drain and set the cauliflower aside.

5. In the pan used for cooking the onion, combine the sauce with the remaining 1 cup of coconut milk. Cover the pan and bring to a boil, about 6 minutes.

6. Add the chili powder, coriander, ground cumin, garam masala, and remaining 1½ teaspoons of salt. Mix and sauté for 1 minute, then stir in the cauliflower and cook for 2 minutes.

7. Mix in the kasuri methi (if using) and remaining ¼ cup of cilantro and remove from the heat.

VARIATION TIP: Instead of cauliflower, you can prepare this same dish with any other vegetable.

PER SERVING: Calories: 282; Total fat: 21g; Saturated fat: 16g; Sodium: 958mg; Carbohydrates: 23g; Sugar: 8g; Fiber: 6g; Protein: 7g

# Palak Ki Kafuli
# (Spinach Curry)

**PREP TIME:** 10 minutes • **COOK TIME:** 15 minutes • **SERVES 4**

Palak kafuli is a recipe from the northern state of Uttarakhand. This dish is very easy to make and is often served as a main course with rice or flatbread. It is healthy, too.

2 tablespoons vegetable oil

¼ teaspoon asafetida (hing)

1 teaspoon cumin seeds

1 teaspoon coriander seeds

1 cup chopped onion

2 green chile peppers, chopped

1 tablespoon ginger paste

1 tablespoon garlic paste

2 tomatoes, finely chopped

1 teaspoon freshly ground black pepper

½ teaspoon salt

1 teaspoon chili powder

1 teaspoon ground coriander

½ teaspoon ground turmeric

1¼ cups water or vegetable broth

3 tablespoons chickpea flour (besan)

8 ounces spinach, finely chopped

1 teaspoon garam masala

1 teaspoon kasuri methi (optional)

1. Heat the oil in a medium kadhai over medium heat. Temper the asafetida, cumin seeds, and coriander seeds. When the seeds crackle, add the onion, green chile peppers, ginger, and garlic. Sauté until the onion turns translucent.

2. Add the tomatoes, black pepper, and salt. Cook until the tomatoes turn soft.

3. Add the chili powder, ground coriander, turmeric, and broth. Cook for 1 minute.

4. Add the chickpea flour and roast until it releases an aroma and the mixture comes together into a dough.

5. Add the spinach and 1 cup of water. Mix and cook for 3 minutes or until the spinach is cooked and the mixture is boiling.

6. Add the garam masala and kasuri methi (if using). Mix and cook for about 30 seconds, then serve.

VARIATION TIP: Instead of spinach, you can use fresh fenugreek leaves or a mix of both. You can also cook the spinach in a pressure cooker and puree it, instead of chopping it. This will increase the cook time and change the texture of the dish.

PER SERVING: Calories: 138; Total fat: 8g; Saturated fat: 1g; Sodium: 366mg; Carbohydrates: 15g; Sugar: 5g; Fiber: 4g; Protein: 4g

# Kerala Avial

**PREP TIME:** 15 minutes • **COOK TIME:** 25 minutes • **SERVES 4**

This version of avial, a popular vegetable dish in the south of India, originates in Kerala. It is said that Bhima, one of the Panadava princes, invented the dish during the thirteenth year of his exile, when he served as a cook to King Virata of the Matsya Kingdom. It is certainly delicious enough to be served to royalty. If you don't have all the vegetables, don't worry; use what you have, and it will still taste great. Serve with steamed rice and sambhar.

⅓ cup peeled and chopped carrots

½ cup cut green beans

1 cup peeled and chopped potatoes

1 cup chopped eggplant

1 cup peeled and chopped chayote

⅓ cup green peas

¾ cup peeled and chopped banana or plantain

10 curry leaves, torn

1½ teaspoons salt

½ teaspoon ground turmeric

1½ teaspoons tamarind paste

1 (13-ounce) can coconut milk

1 cup unsweetened shredded coconut

1 teaspoon cumin seeds

3 green chile peppers

1 tablespoon coconut oil

1. In a pot, bring ½ cup of water to a boil over medium heat. Add the carrots, green beans, and potatoes. Cover the pot and cook for 5 minutes.

2. Add the eggplant, chayote, green peas, banana, curry leaves, salt, turmeric, tamarind paste, and coconut milk. Mix, cover, and cook for 10 minutes or until the vegetables are soft enough to cut with a spoon.

3. While the veggies are cooking, in a blender, combine the coconut, cumin, green chile peppers, and ¼ cup of water. Blend to a smooth paste.

4. Once the veggies are cooked, add the paste and ¼ cup of water to the pot. Mix and cook for another 5 minutes.

5. Lightly stir in the coconut oil and serve.

PER SERVING: Calories: 407; Total fat: 31g; Saturated fat: 27g; Sodium: 905mg; Carbohydrates: 33g; Sugar: 12g; Fiber: 7g; Protein: 6g

# Mushroom Potato Vindaloo

**PREP TIME:** 15 minutes • **COOK TIME:** 25 minutes • **SERVES 4**

Vindaloo is a popular Goan recipe that's usually made with pork marinated in wine. Meaty mushrooms and potatoes are the perfect vegan substitutes. The key to this recipe is the specially made vindaloo masala. Serve with any flatbread or rice.

---

- 4 dried red chile peppers
- 1 tablespoon coriander seeds
- 1 tablespoon cumin seeds
- 5 cloves
- 5 black peppercorns
- 1 cardamom pod
- ¼ teaspoon ground turmeric
- 1 tablespoon rice vinegar
- 2 tablespoons vegetable oil
- 2 potatoes, peeled and cut in medium cubes
- 1½ teaspoons salt, divided
- 1 cup chopped onion
- 1 tablespoon ginger-garlic paste
- 12 ounces mushrooms (any variety), sliced
- ½ teaspoon sugar
- 3 tablespoons chopped fresh cilantro

---

1. In a food processor or mixer grinder, process the red chile peppers, coriander seeds, cumin seeds, cloves, peppercorns, cardamom, turmeric, vinegar, and 2 tablespoons of water. Set the masala aside.

2. Heat the oil in a pan over medium heat. Fry the potato cubes with ½ teaspoon of salt for 12 minutes or until they turn crisp, tossing frequently so they cook evenly. When cooked, transfer to a plate and set aside.

3. In the same pan, sauté the onion with the ginger-garlic paste over medium heat until translucent. Add the mushrooms and sauté for 6 minutes or until the mushrooms are cooked.

4. Add the masala and fry for 30 seconds, then add 1 cup of water, the potatoes, the sugar, and the remaining 1 teaspoon of salt. Mix well, cover, and cook for 6 minutes. Stir in the cilantro and serve.

PER SERVING: Calories: 254; Total fat: 8g; Saturated fat: 1g; Sodium: 893mg; Carbohydrates: 41g; Sugar: 6g; Fiber: 7g; Protein: 7g

# Tofu Saag (Vegan Palak Paneer)

**PREP TIME:** 20 minutes • **COOK TIME:** 15 minutes • **SERVES 4**

Palak paneer is a restaurant favorite for vegetarians, and tofu saag is a vegan take on this classic dish. Here, marinated and grilled tofu is tossed in a mildly spiced spinach gravy. Often served with naan or roti, this gravy doesn't just look appetizing, it is also very nourishing and tasty. If you like (and you probably will), you can drizzle the finished dish with cashew cream or coconut cream.

- 1 teaspoon nutritional yeast
- 1 teaspoon garam masala
- 1 teaspoon garlic powder
- 2 teaspoons salt, divided
- 1 (14-ounce) package tofu, drained and cubed
- 9 ounces spinach
- 2 serrano peppers, coarsely chopped
- 1 teaspoon vegetable oil
- ½ teaspoon cumin seeds
- 1 bay leaf
- 1 tablespoon garlic paste
- 1 tablespoon ginger paste
- 1 cup finely chopped onion
- 1 teaspoon kasuri methi (optional)
- 1 teaspoon ground turmeric
- 1 teaspoon ground coriander
- 1 teaspoon ground cumin
- 1 teaspoon freshly squeezed lemon juice
- ¼ cup chopped fresh cilantro

1. In a medium bowl, combine the nutritional yeast, garam masala, garlic powder, and 1 teaspoon salt. Add the tofu and toss well to evenly coat with the masala. Set aside.

2. Fill a medium pot with water and bring to a boil. Fill a bowl with ice cubes and cold water.

3. Add the spinach and remaining 1 teaspoon salt to the boiling water and let the spinach blanch for 2 minutes. Using tongs or a slotted spoon, transfer the spinach to an ice bath. Let soak for 5 minutes.

4. Drain the spinach and transfer to a food processor. Add the serrano peppers and ½ cup water and blend to a puree.

5. Heat the oil in a pan over medium heat, then temper the cumin seeds, bay leaf, garlic paste, ginger paste, and onion. Sauté until the onion softens.

6. Stir in the kasuri methi (if using), turmeric, coriander, and ground cumin.

7. Add the spinach puree and ⅓ cup of water and cook for 5 minutes.

8. Add the tofu cubes, lemon juice, and cilantro and mix everything well.

PREP TIP: Keep ½ cup of water handy to splash into the pan after adding the spinach in the event it seems dry or the masala is sticking to the pan.

PER SERVING: Calories: 202; Total fat: 10g; Saturated fat: 2g; Sodium: 651mg; Carbohydrates: 14g; Sugar: 3g; Fiber: 5g; Protein: 19g

# Hyderabadi Nizami Handi
# (Mixed Vegetable Curry)

**PREP TIME:** 15 minutes • **COOK TIME:** 45 minutes • **SERVES 6**

Hyderabadi cuisine is known for its meat dishes, which are cooked with spices and herbs. The cuisine is also heavily influenced by Moghul, Arabic, and Turkish cuisines. This dish is a flavorful mixed vegetable curry in a special creamy sauce. *Nizami* means that this dish was prepared in the royal kitchens when the Nizams ruled Hyderabad. *Handi* refers to the clay or copper pot in which the dish used to be made. Serve with any rice or flatbread to soak up the sauce.

3 teaspoons sea salt, divided

1½ teaspoons ground turmeric, divided

2½ cups cauliflower florets

2 potatoes, peeled and cut in cubes

¾ cup chopped carrots

½ cup cut green beans

½ cup green peas

2½ tablespoons vegetable oil

½ bell pepper (any color), coarsely chopped

6 garlic cloves

1 inch ginger

3 green chile peppers

2 tablespoons cashews

1 teaspoon cumin seeds

½ teaspoon ajwain or carom seeds (optional)

1 bay leaf

1 cinnamon stick

1 cardamom pod

1 tablespoon ginger-garlic paste

1 cup finely chopped onion

5 tomatoes, coarsely chopped

1 teaspoon chili powder

1 teaspoon ground coriander

1 teaspoon ground cumin

1 teaspoon garam masala

½ cup cashew paste (see tip) or tahini

1 tablespoon kasuri methi (optional)

3 tablespoons finely chopped fresh cilantro

1. Fill a large pot with water and add 1 teaspoon of salt and 1 teaspoon of turmeric. Cover the pot and bring to a boil over medium heat. Add the cauliflower and potatoes, cover, and boil for 6 minutes.

2. Add the carrots, green beans, and green peas, cover, and boil for another 5 minutes. Place a colander over another pot or a heatproof bowl and drain the veggies, reserving the cooking water.

3. Add ½ tablespoon of oil to the now-empty pot and heat over medium heat. Sauté the bell pepper, garlic, ginger, green chiles, cashews, and 1 teaspoon of salt for 1 minute.

4. Add 1½ cups of reserved cooking water. Cover and cook for 15 minutes.

5. Take the pot off the heat and let cool. Transfer the contents to a food processor and process to a smooth puree. Set aside.

6. In the same pot, heat the remaining 2 tablespoons of oil. Fry the cumin seeds, ajwain (if using), bay leaf, cinnamon, and cardamom for 30 seconds. Add the ginger-garlic paste and onion and sauté until the onion turns translucent.

7. Add the tomatoes and remaining 1 teaspoon of salt. Cook until the tomatoes turn soft and pulpy.

8. Add the chili powder, coriander, ground cumin, garam masala, and remaining ½ teaspoon of turmeric. Sauté for 30 seconds, then add the cashew paste. Mix well and sauté for 3 minutes or until it comes to a boil.

9. Add the bell pepper puree and ½ cup of reserved cooking water. Mix well and cook for another 4 minutes.

10. Stir the boiled veggies into the sauce and cook for 4 minutes, then stir in the kasuri methi (if using) and cilantro. Serve.

PREP TIP: To prepare the cashew paste, soak 1 cup of cashews in hot water for 15 minutes. Drain, then grind the cashews to a smooth paste.

PER SERVING: Calories: 365; Total fat: 19g; Saturated fat: 2g; Sodium: 467mg; Carbohydrates: 44g; Sugar: 9g; Fiber: 10g; Protein: 10g

# Makai Nu Shaak
# (Sweet Corn Curry)

**PREP TIME:** 15 minutes • **COOK TIME:** 20 minutes • **SERVES 4**

This delicious corn curry is from Gujrati cuisine. In this unique recipe, corn is used in three different ways: flavored corn-on-the-cob mini ears, sweet corn kernels in the gravy, and corn paste. This mildly sweet and spicy recipe is excellent for lunch, served with any flatbread or rice.

6 frozen corn-on-the-cob mini ears

1 cup sweet corn kernels, thawed if frozen, divided

5 ounces onion, coarsely chopped

6 garlic cloves

1 inch ginger

1 tablespoon vegan butter

1 tablespoon vegetable oil

1 teaspoon cumin seeds

5 cloves

1-inch cinnamon stick

2 bay leaves

2 dried red chile peppers

2 large tomatoes, pureed

2 teaspoons chili powder

1 teaspoon ground coriander

1 teaspoon garam masala

1 teaspoon kasuri methi (optional)

½ teaspoon ground turmeric

1 teaspoon salt

1 teaspoon sugar

1 potato, cooked, peeled, and mashed

2 tablespoons tahini or cashew paste (see tip on page 101)

¼ cup chopped fresh cilantro

1. Fill a medium pot with water and bring to a boil. Cook the corn-on-the-cob mini ears for 5 minutes, then drain.

2. Process half of the sweet corn in a food processor to a coarse paste. Transfer to a bowl.

3. In the food processor, blend the onion, garlic, and ginger to a smooth paste.

4. In a medium kadhai, heat the butter and oil over medium heat. Temper the cumin seeds, and when they crackle, add the cloves, cinnamon, bay leaves, and dried red chiles and sauté for 30 seconds.

5. Add the onion paste and sauté for 1 minute. Add the tomato puree, mix well, and continue to sauté for 2 more minutes.

6. Stir in the chili powder, coriander, garam masala, kasuri methi (if using), and turmeric and sauté for 5 minutes.

7. Add the salt and sugar, then the corn paste, mashed potato, and tahini. Stir it all together, pour in ¾ cup water, and bring to a boil.

8. Add the remaining sweet corn and mini corn-on-the-cobs. Stir to ensure the ears are coated well with the masala, and cook for an additional 4 minutes. Stir in the cilantro and serve.

PER SERVING: Calories: 288; Total fat: 11g; Saturated fat: 2g; Sodium: 665mg; Carbohydrates: 46g; Sugar: 6g; Fiber: 7g; Protein: 7g

# Kofta Curry with Vegan Meatballs

**PREP TIME:** 15 minutes • **COOK TIME:** 25 minutes • **SERVES 4**

Kofta refers to a spiced meatball, and in this dish the koftas are cooked in a creamy sauce. This recipe can be somewhat elaborate because the koftas need to be made, fried, and then added to the prepared gravy. However, here we will be using store-bought vegan meatballs, to not only save time but also ensure this recipe is fully vegan. Serve with Jeera Garlic Rice (page 67) or any flatbread.

---

- 2 tablespoons vegetable oil, divided
- 1 red bell pepper, coarsely chopped
- 2 tomatoes, coarsely chopped
- 6 garlic cloves, finely chopped
- 3 green chile peppers, finely chopped
- ½ teaspoon sea salt
- 1 teaspoon cumin seeds
- 2 bay leaves
- 1 tablespoon ginger-garlic paste
- 12 frozen vegan meatballs (no need to thaw)
- 2 tablespoons finely chopped fresh mint
- 3 tablespoons finely chopped fresh cilantro

---

1. Heat 1 tablespoon of oil in a medium kadhai over medium heat. Add the bell pepper, tomatoes, garlic, green chile peppers, and salt and fry for 5 minutes. When the veggies are cooked, take the pan off the heat and let cool.

2. In a food processor or mixer grinder, process the veggies to a smooth paste and set aside.

3. Heat the remaining 1 tablespoon of oil in the same kadhai. Temper the cumin seeds. When they crackle, add the bay leaves and ginger-garlic paste. Fry for 30 seconds.

4. Add the veggie paste, 2 cups of water, the frozen meatballs, and the mint. Cover and cook for 16 minutes.

5. When the meatballs are cooked, stir in the cilantro and serve.

PER SERVING: Calories: 194; Total fat: 11g; Saturated fat: 1g; Sodium: 547mg; Carbohydrates: 13g; Sugar: 5g; Fiber: 4g; Protein: 11g

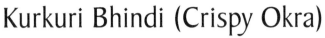

# Kurkuri Bhindi (Crispy Okra)

**PREP TIME:** 20 minutes, plus 30 minutes to marinate
**COOK TIME:** 20 minutes • **SERVES 4**

This recipe is a great way to cook okra. Here, the okra is marinated in a special masala and then fried to give it a crispy-crunchy texture. This is a popular side dish from North Indian cuisine and is a restaurant favorite. You can make it as spicy as you like by adjusting the amount of chili powder.

12 ounces fresh okra, trimmed and cut into long, thin strips

3 tablespoons chickpea flour (besan)

1 to 3 teaspoons chili powder

1 teaspoon ground turmeric

1 teaspoon amchur powder

1 teaspoon onion powder

1 teaspoon garlic powder

1 teaspoon sesame seeds

1 teaspoon salt

1 teaspoon vegetable oil, plus more for deep-frying

1. In a large bowl, combine the okra, chickpea flour, chili powder, turmeric, amchur, onion powder, garlic powder, sesame seeds, salt, and oil.

2. Toss everything together so the okra is well coated with the masala. Set aside to marinate for 30 minutes.

3. Heat some oil for deep-frying in a large pot over medium heat. Add the okra strips and fry until they turn crisp and golden.

4. Transfer the fried okra to a paper towel–lined plate to soak up any excess oil.

**VARIATION TIP:** Instead of deep-frying the okra, you can cook them in an air fryer or bake at 400°F for about 20 minutes.

PER SERVING: Calories: 68; Total fat: 2g; Saturated fat: 0g; Sodium: 68mg; Carbohydrates: 11g; Sugar: 2g; Fiber: 4g; Protein: 3g

# Mushroom Kalan

**PREP TIME:** 10 minutes, plus 20 minutes to marinate • **COOK TIME:** 30 minutes
**SERVES 4**

This unique stir-fry recipe hails from Coimbatore, a city in Tamil Nadu, where it is a popular street food. The mushrooms are coated with a special batter, deep-fried, and then tossed in a sauce made from freshly ground spices. The mushrooms can also be panfried, if you want to use less oil. Fry in small batches so as to not crowd the pan. Serve with bread or paratha.

---

- 6 tablespoons chickpea flour (besan)
- 3 tablespoons rice flour
- 1 tablespoon ginger paste
- 1 tablespoon garlic paste
- 1 tablespoon chili-garlic sauce
- 1 teaspoon ground coriander
- 1 teaspoon ground cumin
- ½ teaspoon ground turmeric
- 1¼ teaspoons salt, divided
- 1¼ pounds mushrooms, sliced
- 5 garlic cloves
- 1 teaspoon cumin seeds
- 1 teaspoon fennel seeds
- 1 teaspoon black peppercorns
- 4 cloves
- 1-inch cinnamon stick
- 2 green chile peppers
- 1 tablespoon vegetable oil, plus more for deep-frying
- 1 cup chopped onion, divided
- ⅓ cup chopped fresh cilantro
- 1 tablespoon freshly squeezed lemon juice

---

1. In a large bowl, combine the chickpea flour, rice flour, ginger paste, garlic paste, chili-garlic sauce, coriander, ground cumin, turmeric, and 1 teaspoon of salt.

2. Add ¾ cup of water gradually to make a smooth, thick, yet flowing batter. Keep stirring to avoid lumps.

3. Add the mushrooms and gently stir to coat them with the batter. Set aside to marinate for 20 minutes.

4. Meanwhile, in a food processor or mixer grinder, combine the garlic, cumin seeds, fennel seeds, peppercorns, cloves, cinnamon, green chile peppers, and ¼ cup of water. Process to a smooth paste and set aside.

5. Heat some oil for deep-frying in a pan over medium-low heat. When the oil is hot, add the mushrooms in small batches and fry, turning once, until golden and crisp on both sides. Transfer to a paper towel–lined plate to soak up any excess oil.

6. Wipe out the pan and add 1 tablespoon of oil. Sauté half the onion over medium heat until translucent. Add the reserved garlic-cumin paste and continue to sauté for 4 minutes.

7. Add the fried mushrooms and remaining ¼ teaspoon of salt and sauté for another 2 minutes.

8. Stir in the cilantro, lemon juice, and remaining onion. Serve.

INGREDIENT TIP: Although any mushroom variety can be used, white mushrooms are preferred.

PER SERVING: Calories: 199; Total fat: 8g; Saturated fat: 1g; Sodium: 804mg; Carbohydrates: 26g; Sugar: 7g; Fiber: 4g; Protein: 8g

# Vegetable Jalfrezi

**PREP TIME:** 15 minutes • **COOK TIME:** 15 minutes • **SERVES 4**

Jalfrezi is a sizzling stir-fried dish loaded with crunchy veggies and meat. This vegan version is spicy and very flavorful. The veggies are stir-fried until somewhat dry, along with chiles to give the dish a pop of heat. Serve this dish with flatbread or rice and a bowl of yogurt on the side, to balance the heat of the spice.

---

2 tablespoons vegan butter

1 cup sliced onion, plus 1 cup minced onion

¾ cup carrot strips

⅓ cup cut green beans

2 cups coarsely chopped tomatoes, plus 2 cups finely chopped tomato

1 teaspoon salt

1 (15-ounce) can baby corn

1 bell pepper (any color), cut in strips

½ cup green peas

2 tablespoons vegetable oil

1 teaspoon cumin seeds

1 teaspoon kasuri methi (optional)

2 green chile peppers, cut into strips

1 tablespoon ginger paste

1 tablespoon garlic paste

1 teaspoon chili powder

1 teaspoon ground coriander

½ teaspoon ground turmeric

2 tablespoons ketchup, tomato paste, or tomato sauce

1 teaspoon garam masala

½ teaspoon freshly ground black pepper

¼ cup chopped fresh cilantro

---

1. Melt the butter in a pan over medium-high heat. Add the chopped onion and sauté for 1 minute, then add the carrots and green beans. Sauté for 4 minutes, then add the coarsely chopped tomatoes and salt. Continue sautéing for 3 minutes.

2. Stir in the baby corn, bell pepper, and green peas and sauté for another 5 minutes.

3. Transfer all the veggies to a bowl and set aside.

4. In the same pan and still over medium heat, heat the oil. Fry the cumin seeds, kasuri methi (if using), green chile peppers, ginger paste, and garlic paste for 1 minute.

5. Add the minced onion and sauté until translucent, then add the finely chopped tomatoes. Cook until soft and pulpy.

6. Stir in the chili powder, coriander, and turmeric and fry for 1 minute.

7. Add the ketchup and stir-fried veggies. Mix and cook for another minute.

8. Stir in the garam masala, black pepper, and cilantro and serve.

PREP TIP: Stir-frying the veggies on slightly high heat helps retain the color and crunch.

PER SERVING: Calories: 290; Total fat: 13g; Saturated fat: 2g; Sodium: 733mg; Carbohydrates: 43g; Sugar: 9g; Fiber: 8g; Protein: 7g

# Dry Dum Aloo
# (Baby Potato Stir-Fry)

**PREP TIME:** 10 minutes • **COOK TIME:** 25 minutes • **SERVES 4**

This delicious dish is made with baby potatoes cooked with a variety of spices. It's a very popular recipe from the north of India and is served on festive occasions. *Dum* in Indian cuisine refers to the technique of cooking the dish in a sealed pot over low heat. Serve with any flatbread.

---

½ cup coarsely chopped onion

6 garlic cloves, peeled

1 tablespoon ginger paste

12 ounces baby potatoes, peeled

4 tablespoons vegetable oil, divided

1 teaspoon salt

3 dried red chile peppers

2 bay leaves

1 teaspoon cumin seeds

¼ teaspoon asafetida (hing)

1 teaspoon ground turmeric

1 teaspoon chili powder

1 teaspoon ground coriander

1 teaspoon garam masala

½ teaspoon chaat masala

¼ cup chopped fresh cilantro

---

1. In a food processor or mixer grinder, process the onion, garlic, and ginger paste to a smooth paste.

2. Prick the peeled potatoes all over with a fork, so they can absorb the masala. Then cut them in half.

3. In a medium kadhai, heat 3 tablespoons of oil over medium heat. Add the salt and potatoes and fry until golden and crisp, about 10 minutes. Transfer to a plate.

4. Heat the remaining 1 tablespoon of oil in the kadhai, still over medium heat. Sauté the dried red chile peppers, bay leaves, cumin seeds, and asafetida for 2 minutes.

5. Add 2 tablespoons of water, the turmeric, chili powder, coriander, and garam masala. Cook for 1 minute.

6. Add the fried potatoes and mix them with the masala. Cover and cook for 8 minutes. Add up to ¼ cup of water if the mixture becomes too dry, or up to 1 cup if you prefer to make a gravy.

7. Add the chaat masala, mix, and continue to cook for another minute.

8. Stir in the cilantro. Take the kadhai off the heat but keep it covered until it's time to serve.

PREP TIP: Instead of baby potatoes, you can use regular-size potatoes, peeled and cut into cubes. After cutting the potatoes, soak them in water till it's time to fry them. This will prevent them from discoloring.

PER SERVING: Calories: 219; Total fat: 14g; Saturated fat: 1g; Sodium: 610mg; Carbohydrates: 21g; Sugar: 3g; Fiber: 2g; Protein: 21g

# Maharashtrian Zunka (Chickpea Flour Mash)

**PREP TIME:** 10 minutes • **COOK TIME:** 15 minutes • **SERVES 4**

This is a popular side dish from Maharashtrian cuisine. Considered to be farmers' food, zunka is prepared with sautéed chickpea flour. The trick to cooking the flour is to work fast. Keep stirring it over low to medium heat, splashing it with water as needed to keep it from getting too dry and sticking.

---

4 tablespoons vegetable oil, divided

1 teaspoon mustard seeds

1 teaspoon cumin seeds

¼ teaspoon asafetida (hing)

6 garlic cloves, crushed

2 green chile peppers, minced

1 cup chopped onion

1 teaspoon chili powder

1 teaspoon garam masala

1 teaspoon salt

½ teaspoon ground turmeric

1½ cups chickpea flour (besan)

2 tablespoons finely chopped fresh cilantro

---

1. Heat 3 tablespoons of oil in a medium kadhai over medium heat. Temper the mustard seeds, cumin seeds, and asafetida. When the mustard seeds crackle, add the garlic, green chile peppers, and onion and sauté until translucent.

2. Add the chili powder, garam masala, salt, and turmeric and sauté for 1 minute.

3. Adjust the heat to medium-low. Add the chickpea flour gradually in four parts, continually stirring the flour into the mixture and adding the next batch when there is no dry flour left.

4. Once all the flour is added, cook for 2 minutes. Add 7 tablespoons of water and the remaining 1 tablespoon of oil. Keep sautéing until the mixture resembles a crumble and the flour is fully cooked with no remaining smell of raw flour.

5. Garnish with the cilantro and serve.

PER SERVING: Calories: 297; Total fat: 17g; Saturated fat: 1g; Sodium: 628mg; Carbohydrates: 28g; Sugar: 7g; Fiber: 5g; Protein: 9g

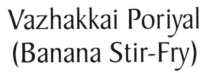

# Vazhakkai Poriyal (Banana Stir-Fry)

**PREP TIME:** 10 minutes • **COOK TIME:** 15 minutes • **SERVES 4**

This recipe is another classic from Tamil Brahmin cuisine (from southern India). It's a simple yet delicious stir-fry that's a great way to enjoy bananas or plantains in everyday cooking. This dish is typically served with sambhar and rice.

2 tablespoons coconut oil

1 teaspoon mustard seeds

1 tablespoon urad dal

¼ teaspoon asafetida (hing)

10 curry leaves

5 bananas or plantains, peeled and cut into medium cubes

3 tablespoons sambhar powder

1 teaspoon salt

2 tablespoons chopped fresh cilantro

1. In a medium kadhai over medium heat, heat the coconut oil. Temper the mustard seeds. When they crackle, add the urad dal, asafetida, and curry leaves. Fry until the lentils turn golden.

2. Stir in the banana cubes, sambhar powder, and salt. Cover and cook, stirring frequently, for 10 minutes. If the mixture gets dry, add 2 tablespoons of water.

3. Once the bananas are cooked, stir in the cilantro and serve.

PREP TIP: Before peeling the bananas, grease your hands with oil to avoid stickiness, and ensure that you peel until the white part is visible. After chopping them, immerse the bananas in water until you need them to stop them from discoloring.

VARIATION TIP: You can add rasam powder or Madras curry powder for a different flavor. You can also skip the sambhar powder, which will result in a milder flavor.

PER SERVING: Calories: 210; Total fat: 7g; Saturated fat: 6g; Sodium: 587mg; Carbohydrates: 38g; Sugar: 18g; Fiber: 5g; Protein: 2g

**Carrot Halwa**
**page 126**

# Drinks and Desserts

# Masala Doodh (Spiced Milk)

**PREP TIME:** 5 minutes • **COOK TIME:** 15 minutes • **SERVES 4**

Masala doodh is a traditional sweetened milk recipe popular in the western state of Maharashtra. The spice mixture can be added to smoothies and desserts, too.

¼ cup raw unsalted almonds

¼ cup raw unsalted cashews

¼ cup raw unsalted pistachios

3 black peppercorns

2 cloves

½ teaspoon saffron strands

¼ teaspoon ground cardamom

⅛ teaspoon ground nutmeg (optional)

3 cups plain unsweetened nondairy milk

¼ cup sugar

1. In a pan, dry-roast the almonds, cashews, pistachios, peppercorns, and cloves over medium heat for 2 minutes or until the nuts brown a bit. Take the pan off the heat and allow to cool.

2. When the nuts have cooled, transfer them to a blender and blend to a fine powder.

3. To make the masala, transfer to a bowl and add the saffron, cardamom, and nutmeg (if using). Stir well and store in an airtight container.

4. To make the spiced milk, pour the milk into a thick-bottomed pan. Bring to a boil over medium heat. Keep stirring the milk regularly.

5. Add the sugar and 3 tablespoons of masala. Stir and cook for another 5 minutes. You can serve this drink hot or cold.

PREP TIP: For best results when roasting nuts, make sure they're completely dry before you start, and keep tossing them to ensure even roasting.

VARIATION TIP: Add ¼ teaspoon ground turmeric to the milk in step 5 to make your own turmeric latte.

PER SERVING: Calories: 257; Total fat: 15g; Saturated fat: 2g; Sodium: 65mg; Carbohydrates: 23g; Sugar: 15g; Fiber: 3g; Protein: 10g

# Masala Chai (Spiced Indian Tea)

**PREP TIME:** 5 minutes • **COOK TIME:** 10 minutes • **SERVES 4**

Masala chai is one of the most-consumed Indian beverages. Indian tea is a frothy, rich, milky, deep-colored, and flavorful beverage. Brew this masala chai at home using whole spices, and enjoy it in the morning, the evening or indeed anytime, ideally with a cookie or biscuit. Always make it fresh and drink it immediately, while hot. Using oat or cashew milk will give you a flavor closest to the traditional.

3 cardamom pods
1 inch ginger, grated
4 cloves

3 black
    peppercorns, crushed
2 tablespoons loose tea

1 cup plain
    unsweetened oat
    or nut milk
4 teaspoons sugar

1. Pour 2 cups of water into a pot over medium heat. Bring to a boil.

2. Add the cardamom, ginger, cloves, and peppercorns, then add the loose tea and boil for 4 minutes.

3. Place 4 small heatproof glasses on a tray. Fill the glasses half full with the tea by passing it through a sieve or strainer.

4. Heat the oat or nut milk in the microwave for 1 minute.

5. Fill the glasses with hot oat or nut milk. Add 1 teaspoon of sugar to each glass.

6. Stir until the sugar dissolves and serve immediately.

**INGREDIENT TIP:** Do not use ginger paste as a substitute for ginger. Skip it if you don't have fresh ginger.

**VARIATION TIP:** If you want to make regular chai, omit the cloves and peppercorns.

PER SERVING: Calories: 36; Total fat: 1g; Saturated fat: 0g; Sodium: 21mg; Carbohydrates: 5g; Sugar: 4g; Fiber: 0g; Protein: 2g

# Surti Cold Cocoa

**PREP TIME:** 5 minutes, plus 5 hours to chill • **COOK TIME:** 20 minutes • **SERVES 6**

This is a very popular cold cocoa drink from Surat, a city in Gujarat. You can beat the heat by making this creamy, smooth, and chilled drink. It may look like a regular chocolate drink, but the unique preparation makes the difference in the taste. It is truly lip-smackingly good. And how about some chocolate shavings or toasted Rice Krispies on top, for extra flavor? Yes? Thought so.

3 tablespoons unsweetened cocoa or cacao powder

1½ tablespoons cornstarch

1½ tablespoons vegan custard powder

4½ cups plain unsweetened nondairy milk, divided

¾ cup sugar

¾ cup nondairy creamer

1. In a bowl, combine the cocoa powder, cornstarch, and custard powder and stir well.

2. Gradually add ½ cup of milk, whisking continuously until smooth and creamy. There should be no lumps.

3. Pour this cocoa mixture into a thick-bottomed pan. Add the remaining 4 cups of milk. Stir and place the pan over medium heat.

4. Stir in the sugar and cook until the sugar dissolves and the milk comes to a boil and thickens, about 15 minutes.

5. Remove the pot from the heat and immediately stir in the creamer. Allow the milk to come to room temperature, then transfer it to the refrigerator and let it chill for at least 5 hours.

6. Put some ice cubes into 6 glasses. Fill the glasses with cocoa milk and serve immediately.

PER SERVING: Calories: 227; Total fat: 7g; Saturated fat: 1g; Sodium: 103mg; Carbohydrates: 34g; Sugar: 26g; Fiber: 2g; Protein: 7g

# Imli Panna (Tamarind Soda)

**PREP TIME:** 5 minutes • **COOK TIME:** 5 minutes • **SERVES 4**

Imli panna soda is a vegan summer cooler that is tangy and sweet. This crowd favorite is super easy to make, tastes great, and is wonderfully refreshing for hot days.

| | | |
|---|---|---|
| 1 cup sugar | ½ teaspoon ground cumin | Soda, chilled |
| ¼ cup tamarind paste | ½ teaspoon black salt | 8 mint leaves |

1. In a thick-bottomed pan over medium heat, combine the sugar and 1½ cups of water. Mix well and cook until the sugar has dissolved.

2. Stir in the tamarind paste and bring to a boil. The mixture will thicken after 10 to 12 minutes; at that point, take the pan off the heat.

3. Let the syrup come to room temperature, then transfer to the refrigerator until it's time to serve.

4. Put some ice cubes into 4 serving glasses, and add ⅛ teaspoon each of cumin and black salt to each glass.

5. Fill one-third of each glass with tamarind syrup. Fill the remainder of the glasses with chilled soda.

6. Garnish with the mint leaves, stir, and serve immediately.

**PREP TIP:** Adjust the sweetness to your taste. Store the tamarind syrup in the refrigerator in an airtight container for up to 6 days. The syrup can also be added to snow cones.

PER SERVING: Calories: 212; Total fat: 0g; Saturated fat: 0g; Sodium: 148mg; Carbohydrates: 55g; Sugar: 53g; Fiber: 0g; Protein: 0g

# Tempered Cucumber Buttermilk

**PREP TIME:** 5 minutes, plus time to chill • **COOK TIME:** 10 minutes • **SERVES 4**

Chaas or buttermilk is one of the most favored drinks in Indian cuisine. It's usually consumed at the end of a meal because it helps with digestion and cools the body. Adding cucumber to this drink makes it even more refreshing and nourishing. The tadka gives this drink an extra zing.

1 cucumber, peeled and coarsely chopped

1 green chile pepper, chopped

¼ cup chopped fresh cilantro

6 mint leaves

1 teaspoon black salt

1 teaspoon ground cumin

1 cup plain unsweetened nondairy yogurt

½ teaspoon salt

1 teaspoon vegetable oil

1 teaspoon cumin seeds

½ teaspoon asafetida (hing)

6 curry leaves, torn into small shreds

1. In a food processor or mixer grinder, combine the cucumber, green chile pepper, cilantro, mint, black salt, and ground cumin. Process to a smooth puree.

2. In a bowl, whisk the yogurt until smooth. Add 2 cups of water, the cucumber puree, and salt. Mix it all together.

3. Heat the oil in a tadka pan over medium heat. Temper the cumin seeds. When they begin to crackle, add the asafetida and curry leaves.

4. Pour this tadka over the buttermilk. Serve chilled.

PREP TIP: Adjust the consistency of the buttermilk to your preference. You can make it thin or thick.

VARIATION TIP: You can also make this buttermilk without the tadka.

PER SERVING: Calories: 67; Total fat: 2g; Saturated fat: 0g; Sodium: 535mg; Carbohydrates: 10g; Sugar: 5g; Fiber: 1g; Protein: 2g

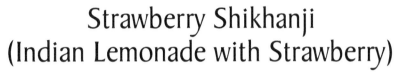

# Strawberry Shikhanji
# (Indian Lemonade with Strawberry)

**PREP TIME:** 5 minutes, plus time to chill • **COOK TIME:** 15 minutes • **SERVES 4**

Shikhanji is an Indian-style spiced lemonade. It's cool, refreshing, and very flavorful. In this recipe, strawberries give it a certain tartness and a beautiful color.

---

5 strawberries,
  coarsely chopped

¼ cup sugar

10 mint leaves

1 teaspoon
  ground cumin

1 teaspoon ground
  coriander

1 teaspoon black salt

Juice of 2 lemons
  or limes

Water or soda, chilled

---

1. In a pan, combine the strawberries, sugar, mint, and ⅓ cup water. Bring to a boil over medium heat, mashing the berries until they break down completely into a smooth consistency.

2. Take the pan off the heat and allow it to cool, then place in the refrigerator.

3. In a bowl, stir together the cumin, coriander, black salt, and lemon juice. Keep in the refrigerator until it's time to serve.

4. To prepare the drinks, put ice cubes in 4 glasses. Pour 1 tablespoon of strawberry mixture followed by 2 tablespoons of lemon juice mixture into each glass.

5. Add chilled water or soda to fill the glasses. Serve immediately.

**VARIATION TIP:** You can swap out the strawberries for blueberries or raspberries.

PER SERVING: Calories: 61; Total fat: 0g; Saturated fat: 0g; Sodium: 234mg; Carbohydrates: 16g; Sugar: 14g; Fiber: 0g; Protein: 0g

# Kaju Katli (Cashew Fudge)

**PREP TIME:** 5 minutes • **COOK TIME:** 20 minutes • **MAKES 16 PIECES**

Kaju katli is a popular Indian fudge. *Kaju* means "cashews" and *katli* means "cut," and in this recipe the pieces are shaped like diamonds. This sweet is prepared for most festivals and on auspicious occasions. This recipe is the vegan version of this classic dessert.

| | | |
|---|---|---|
| 1 cup raw<br>  unsalted cashews<br>½ cup sugar | ¼ teaspoon<br>  cardamom powder | ½ teaspoon<br>  saffron strands |

1. Grease and line an 8-inch baking dish.

2. In a food processor or mixer grinder, process the cashews to a fine powder. Transfer to a bowl and set aside.

3. In a thick-bottomed pan, combine the sugar and ¼ cup of water. Cook over medium heat for 10 minutes or until the syrup achieves a one-thread consistency (see tip). Take the pan off the heat.

4. In a separate pan, dry-roast the cashew powder over medium heat for 2 minutes. Keep tossing the powder to ensure even roasting.

5. Add the cardamom and saffron and mix well. Add the sugar syrup and quickly mix everything together.

6. Cook until the mixture comes together and does not stick to the pan anymore. Transfer to the prepared dish and flatten it to a ¼-inch thickness.

7. Let it cool to room temperature and then cut into diamond-shape pieces.

**PREP TIPS:** Do not grind the cashews for long or else they will begin to release their oils. Just pulse them until they turn to powder. To check the one-thread consistency, place a drop of the sugar syrup on the tip of your thumb and touch the tip of your forefinger to it. The syrup should stretch into a short thread as you separate your thumb and forefinger.

PER SERVING (1 PIECE): Calories: 76; Total fat: 4g; Saturated fat: 1g; Sodium: 1mg; Carbohydrates: 9g; Sugar: 7g; Fiber: 0g; Protein: 2g

# Coconut Milk Fruit Custard

**PREP TIME:** 5 minutes • **COOK TIME:** 15 minutes • **SERVES 6**

Fruit custard is made in nearly every Indian home. Traditionally, custard is prepared with cream and eggs, but to make it vegan, we use coconut milk, which gives this custard a very nice flavor. Use coconut milk from a carton for this recipe, as it is thinner than milk from a can. But if all you have is canned, just thin it with some water and enjoy a thick, creamy, and luscious dessert that's perfect for any occasion.

3 tablespoons cornstarch or vegan custard powder

2¼ cups coconut milk from a carton, divided

⅓ cup sugar

1 teaspoon vanilla extract

1 cup chopped mixed fruits (such as apple, banana, mango, or kiwi)

¼ teaspoon ground cardamom

1. In a small bowl, mix the cornstarch with ¼ cup of coconut milk in a small bowl until completely lump-free. Set aside.

2. In a thick-bottomed pan over medium heat, combine the remaining 2 cups of coconut milk, sugar, and vanilla. Add the cornstarch mixture. Mix and cook for 10 minutes or until the mixture thickens. Take it off the heat and transfer to a bowl to cool completely.

3. When cool, stir in the mixed fruits and cardamom. Refrigerate until it's time to serve.

**VARIATION TIP:** You can serve this coconut milk custard without the fruit. To make it more fun for kids, drizzle some chocolate syrup on top and serve.

PER SERVING: Calories: 113; Total fat: 1g; Saturated fat: 0g; Sodium: 37mg; Carbohydrates: 25g; Sugar: 18g; Fiber: 1g; Protein: 1g

# Jhajhariya (Sweet Corn Pudding)

**PREP TIME:** 10 minutes • **COOK TIME:** 15 minutes • **SERVES 6**

Jhajjhariya is a delicious sweet corn pudding from the north of India. This recipe is a veganized version of the popular dessert. It's easy and quick to make and has just a few ingredients. The pudding thickens as it cools.

| | | |
|---|---|---|
| 3 cups sweet corn, thawed if frozen | 1 cup coconut milk from a carton | ¼ teaspoon saffron strands |
| ¼ cup coconut oil | ½ cup sugar | 2 tablespoons sliced almonds |
| | ½ cup almond flour | |

1. In a food processor or mixer grinder, process the corn coarsely.

2. Heat the coconut oil in a pan over medium heat. Sauté the corn for 4 minutes, tossing continuously to ensure even cooking.

3. Stir in the coconut milk and cook for 5 minutes, then add the sugar. Continue to cook for another 4 minutes or until the mixture thickens a bit.

4. Stir in the almond flour. This will thicken the mixture. Cook for 2 minutes.

5. Garnish with the saffron and almond slices. Serve warm or chilled.

PER SERVING: Calories: 296; Total fat: 15g; Saturated fat: 5g; Sodium: 19mg; Carbohydrates: 39g; Sugar: 17g; Fiber: 4g; Protein: 6g

# Kesar Pista Ice Cream

**PREP TIME:** 10 minutes, plus 8 hours to freeze • **COOK TIME:** 10 minutes • **SERVES 4**

This is a very popular ice cream flavor in India. *Kesar* means "saffron" and *pista* means "pistachios." They make a great combo in many Indian desserts. This ice cream recipe does not require an ice cream maker. You can also pour this mixture into ice pop molds.

2¼ cups plain unsweetened nondairy milk or creamer, divided

½ teaspoon saffron strands

⅓ cup sugar

⅛ teaspoon salt

½ cup almond butter or nut butter of choice

¼ cup pistachios, finely chopped

1. Pour ¼ cup of milk into a small bowl. Add the saffron and let it steep for 10 minutes.

2. In a blender, combine the remaining 2 cups of milk and, the sugar, salt, almond butter, pistachios, and saffron milk. Blitz until smooth and creamy.

3. Transfer to an airtight freezer-safe container. Leave it in the freezer overnight.

**PREP TIP:** The consistency of the ice cream batter should be smooth and creamy after blending. You can also mix in the chopped nuts instead of grinding them, to give it some crunch.

PER SERVING: Calories: 344; Total fat: 23g; Saturated fat: 2g; Sodium: 128mg; Carbohydrates: 27g; Sugar: 19g; Fiber: 5g; Protein: 12g

# Carrot Halwa

**PREP TIME:** 10 minutes • **COOK TIME:** 40 minutes • **SERVES 6**

Indian festivals are incomplete without carrot halwa. This delicious creamy carrot pudding is normally prepared with milk. However, this vegan recipe is prepared with almond flour and nondairy creamer. Serve the halwa with ice cream for a popular and delicious combo.

2 tablespoons coconut oil

½ cup mixed nuts and dried fruits (such as cashews, almonds, pistachios, and raisins)

6 cups peeled and grated carrots

3 cups plain unsweetened nondairy creamer

¼ teaspoon ground cardamom

⅛ teaspoon salt

¾ cup powdered sugar or jaggery powder

1 cup almond flour

1. Heat the coconut oil in a pan over medium heat. Fry the nuts and dried fruits for 2 minutes. Transfer to a plate.

2. In the same pan (no need to wipe out the oil), sauté the carrots for 5 minutes, tossing regularly so they cook evenly.

3. Add the creamer, stir, and continue to cook for 15 minutes or until the carrots are soft and fully cooked.

4. Add the cardamom, salt, and sugar. Mix and cook for another 5 minutes.

5. Add the almond flour. Mix and cook for 5 minutes or until the halwa thickens and doesn't stick to the pan.

6. Stir in the dried nuts and fruits and take the pan off the heat. Serve hot or chilled.

VARIATION TIP: **Try using grated beet instead of carrot for a twist on this classic.**

PER SERVING: Calories: 381; Total fat: 21g; Saturated fat: 5g; Sodium: 210mg; Carbohydrates: 44g; Sugar: 25g; Fiber: 6g; Protein: 5g

# Apple Coconut Barfi

**PREP TIME:** 10 minutes, plus 2 hours to chill • **COOK TIME:** 20 minutes

**MAKES 12 PIECES**

Barfi is a soft and chewy bite-size dessert that is normally prepared with milk and milk solids. Here, the barfi is prepared with apples and coconuts, which give this dessert a unique flavor. This dessert is great for gifting and for all festive occasions.

---

4 sweet apples, peeled, cored, and grated

1½ cups sugar

1 cup unsweetened shredded coconut

½ cup chopped walnuts or macadamia nuts

¼ teaspoon ground cardamom

2 tablespoons chopped pistachios

---

1. Grease and line an 8-inch baking dish.

2. In a thick-bottomed pan, combine the apples, sugar, and coconut and cook over medium heat for 10 minutes or until the apples are cooked.

3. Add the walnuts and cardamom. Cook for another 5 minutes, stirring continuously and scraping the sides of the pan to prevent sticking. The mixture should come together and pull away from the sides of the pan.

4. Transfer the mixture to the prepared baking dish. Spread and flatten it.

5. Scatter the pistachios on top and press them lightly into the mixture.

6. Let it cool a bit and then cut into 12 slices. Refrigerate for at least 2 hours before serving.

PER SERVING (1 PIECE): Calories: 199; Total fat: 7g; Saturated fat: 3g; Sodium: 2mg; Carbohydrates: 35g; Sugar: 32g; Fiber: 3g; Protein: 1g

# Besan Nankhatai (Indian Cookies)

**PREP TIME:** 15 minutes • **COOK TIME:** 15 minutes • **MAKES 14 COOKIES**

Besan nankhatai is a vegan version of regular nankhatai, which are also known as milk cookies. These delicious Indian-style shortbread cookies are light and crumbly and will melt in your mouth.

½ cup chickpea
   flour (besan)

½ cup whole wheat flour

¾ teaspoon baking soda

¼ teaspoon ground
   cardamom

Pinch salt

½ cup jaggery powder
   or powdered sugar

½ cup vegetable oil

Sliced almonds,
   for garnish

1. Preheat the oven to 350°F. Line a rimmed baking sheet with parchment paper.

2. Sift the chickpea and wheat flours into a bowl. Add the baking soda, cardamom, and salt. Mix it all together.

3. In another bowl, combine the jaggery powder, oil, and 2 tablespoons of water. Whisk together until smooth and creamy.

4. Pour the jaggery sauce over the flour and fold the mixture until there is no dry flour left and a soft dough has formed. Cover with plastic wrap and let rest for 10 minutes.

5. Cut the dough into 14 pieces and shape into golf-ball–size balls. Flatten lightly. Lightly press 2 or 3 almond slices onto each cookie.

6. Place the pieces on the prepared baking sheet, leaving a few inches between the cookies. Bake for 15 minutes.

7. Remove from the oven and allow to cool for 10 minutes or until they harden. Store in an airtight container.

**PREP TIP:** Do not knead the dough. Just fold the mixture until it's well combined.

PER SERVING (1 COOKIE): Calories: 121; Total fat: 9g; Saturated fat: 1g; Sodium: 82mg; Carbohydrates: 9g; Sugar: 4g; Fiber: 1g; Protein: 2g

# Paal Payasam (Rice Pudding)

**PREP TIME:** 5 minutes • **COOK TIME:** 45 minutes • **SERVES 4**

Paal payasam, also known as rice pudding or kheer, is a South Indian delicacy. This thick and creamy dessert is served on all happy and festive occasions. This recipe is a veganized version of the traditional milk-based dessert. To switch it up, try making it with vermicelli instead of rice.

1 tablespoon coconut oil

2 tablespoons uncooked rice

2 cups plain unsweetened nondairy milk

3 tablespoons powdered sugar or jaggery powder

½ teaspoon saffron strands

1 tablespoon almond slices

1. Heat the oil in a thick-bottomed pan over medium heat. Lightly roast the rice for 3 minutes.

2. Add the milk and cook, stirring frequently, until the milk reduces and thickens and the rice is cooked, about 30 minutes.

3. Stir in the sugar and continue to cook for another 10 minutes.

4. Add the saffron and almond slices, stir, and take the pan off the heat.

5. Serve hot or chilled.

PREP TIP: Roasting the rice first gives it a nice, toasty flavor. Stirring the milk with rice in it helps prevent the rice from sticking to the bottom of the pan. To check if the rice is cooked, crush the rice with the back of a ladle. If it crushes easily, the rice is cooked.

PER SERVING: Calories: 124; Total fat: 6g; Saturated fat: 3g; Sodium: 43mg; Carbohydrates: 13g; Sugar: 6g; Fiber: 1g; Protein: 4g

# Almond Flour Ladoos

**PREP TIME:** 5 minutes • **COOK TIME:** 10 minutes • **MAKES 12 LADOOS**

Indian celebrations are incomplete without ladoos. Each region has its own variation. This dessert is normally made with ghee, but here we use coconut oil to make it vegan. These no-cook treats are quick and easy to make. A fun twist is to add some colored food dye.

1 cup blanched almond flour

¼ cup unsweetened shredded coconut

½ cup powdered sugar

¼ teaspoon ground cardamom

¼ cup warm coconut oil

1. In a bowl, stir together the almond flour and coconut, then add the powdered sugar and cardamom.

2. Add the warm coconut oil and stir well until the mixture becomes crumbly in texture.

3. Grease your palms with a little oil to prevent the mixture from sticking to your hands, then shape into 12 small balls. You'll need to squeeze them hard with your palms to get the desired shape. Store the ladoos in an airtight container.

PER SERVING (1 LADOO): Calories: 107; Total fat: 9g; Saturated fat: 5g; Sodium: 1mg; Carbohydrates: 6g; Sugar: 4g; Fiber: 1g; Protein: 2g

**TVP-Stuffed Flatbread**
**page 150**

# Basics and Flatbreads

# Burani Raita
# (Tempered Yogurt Dip)

**PREP TIME:** 5 minutes • **COOK TIME:** 5 minutes • **MAKES ABOUT 2 CUPS**

Burani raita is a spiced yogurt dip flavored with a tempering of garlic. The recipe hails from Hyderabadi cuisine and is a very flavorful accompaniment for rice and curry dishes such as biryani.

2 cups plain unsweetened nondairy yogurt

1 teaspoon chili powder

1 teaspoon black salt

1 teaspoon ground cumin

1 teaspoon vegetable oil

1 teaspoon mustard seeds

6 garlic cloves, minced

5 curry leaves

½ green chile pepper, minced

6 mint leaves

2 tablespoons chopped fresh cilantro

1. Put the yogurt in a medium bowl and whisk it while adding ½ cup of water.

2. Add the chili powder, black salt, and cumin. Mix well and set aside.

3. Heat the oil in a tadka pan over medium heat. Temper the mustard seeds. When they crackle, add the garlic, curry leaves, and green chile pepper.

4. Pour the tadka over the yogurt mixture.

5. Add the mint and cilantro and mix well. Keep the raita chilled until it's time to serve.

**VARIATION TIP:** For more flavor, add some veggies like onions, cucumbers, carrots, and tomatoes.

PER SERVING (¼ CUP): Calories: 50; Total fat: 2g; Saturated fat: 0g; Sodium: 134mg; Carbohydrates: 7g; Sugar: 3g; Fiber: 1g; Protein: 2g

# Maharashtrian Thecha
# (Spicy Peanut Garlic Chutney)

**PREP TIME:** 5 minutes • **COOK TIME:** 15 minutes • **MAKES ABOUT 1 CUP**

Thecha is a spicy chutney often served with bhakhri. *Thecha* means "crushed," and this chutney is prepared by crushing the ingredients, which releases a unique flavor. Serve as an accompaniment with flatbread or bread.

---

3 tablespoons vegetable oil, divided

10 garlic cloves, coarsely chopped

10 green chile peppers or 6 serrano peppers, coarsely chopped

½ cup peanuts

¼ cup unsweetened shredded coconut

½ teaspoon salt

---

1. Heat 1 tablespoon of oil in a pan over medium heat. Fry the garlic and green chile peppers for 30 seconds.

2. Reduce the heat slightly and add the peanuts and coconut. Sauté for 10 minutes, tossing everything to ensure even roasting and avoid burning.

3. Take the pan off the heat and allow the contents to cool completely.

4. Transfer the mixture to a food processor or mixer grinder and process coarsely.

5. Heat the remaining 2 tablespoons of oil in the same pan over medium heat. Sauté the ground mixture for 4 minutes, then stir in the salt. Mix well.

**PREP TIP:** Instead of a mixer grinder, you can also crush the ingredients using a mortar and pestle, which is how it's traditionally done.

**VARIATION TIP:** If the heat is too much, mix it with vegan butter to make your own flavored butter.

PER SERVING (2 TABLESPOONS): Calories: 135; Total fat: 11g; Saturated fat: 2g; Sodium: 151mg; Carbohydrates: 8g; Sugar: 3g; Fiber: 2g; Protein: 4g

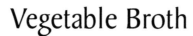

# Vegetable Broth

This is the perfect way to put vegetable scraps to good use. This delicious broth can be used in any savory recipe that calls for water. It is so much better than store-bought broth because it is sodium free and contains no preservatives or no artificial flavors. Save peels, stalks, and vegetable ends in a freezer-safe bag or container until you have enough to make a batch of this broth. You can also use the water left over from boiling lentils, legumes, or veggies.

3 cups vegetable scraps

2 bay leaves

1 teaspoon
 garlic powder

1 teaspoon
 onion powder

1 teaspoon
 ground cumin

½ teaspoon ground
 turmeric

1. In a large pot, combine the vegetable scraps, 6 cups of water, the bay leaves, garlic powder, onion powder, cumin, and turmeric. Cover the pot and bring to a boil over medium heat. Reduce the heat and let simmer for 30 minutes, stirring occasionally.

2. Take the pot off the heat and allow the broth to cool completely.

3. Strain the broth into a glass bottle or jar. Store in the refrigerator.

**VARIATION TIP:** You can make plain broth by simply omitting the spices.

PER SERVING (1 CUP): Calories: 15; Total fat: 0g; Saturated fat: 0g; Sodium: 15mg; Carbohydrates: 3g; Sugar: 0g; Fiber: 0g; Protein: 0g

# Sambhar Powder

**PREP TIME:** 5 minutes • **COOK TIME:** 10 minutes • **MAKES ABOUT 3 CUPS**

Sambhar powder is a South Indian spice mix that's used in stews and curries and even added to flavored rice. It can be made in advance and stored for months, so stock up and always have some on hand; you'll be glad you did.

---

1 cup dried red
  chile peppers
2 cups coriander seeds
½ cup tur dal

¼ cup chana dal
1 tablespoon
  methi seeds

1 teaspoon
  asafetida (hing)
10 black peppercorns
¼ cup ground turmeric

---

1. In a pan, dry-roast the red chile peppers over medium heat for 3 minutes or until they turn a shade darker. Transfer to a bowl and set aside.

2. In the same pan, dry-roast the coriander seeds for 3 minutes. Transfer to a separate bowl and set aside.

3. In the same pan, dry-roast the tur dal, chana dal, methi seeds, asafetida, and peppercorns together for 3 minutes. Transfer to the bowl with the coriander.

4. Allow everything to cool completely.

5. When cool, in a food processor or mixer grinder, process the red chile peppers to a fine powder. Transfer to a large bowl.

6. Pour the coriander and dal mixture into the food processor and process to a coarse powder. Transfer to the bowl with the chile pepper powder.

7. Add the turmeric and mix everything together well.

PER SERVING (1 TABLESPOON): Calories: 29; Total fat: 1g; Saturated fat: 0g; Sodium: 3mg; Carbohydrates: 6g; Sugar: 1g; Fiber: 3g; Protein: 2g

# Green Chutney

**PREP TIME:** 5 minutes • **COOK TIME:** 5 minutes • **MAKES ABOUT 1 CUP**

Green chutney is a spicy condiment prepared with cilantro and mint leaves. This chutney is served as a side for appetizers, snacks, and even parathas. This simple-to-prepare chutney can be whipped up in just 10 minutes. Freeze the chutney in ice cube trays for ease of use.

2 bunches fresh cilantro, bottom 2 inches of stems removed

1 cup mint leaves

3 tablespoons peanuts

5 garlic cloves, peeled

½ inch ginger, peeled

2 green chile peppers

1 tablespoon freshly squeezed lemon juice

1 teaspoon cumin seeds

½ teaspoon salt

¼ teaspoon sugar

4 ice cubes

1. In a food processor or mixer grinder, combine the cilantro, mint, peanuts, garlic, ginger, green chile peppers, lemon juice, cumin, salt, and sugar.

2. Add 3 tablespoons of chilled water and the ice cubes. Blitz to make a smooth puree.

3. Transfer to a bowl. Check and adjust the salt as needed.

4. Store in the refrigerator for up to 4 days. It also freezes well.

**PREP TIP:** Chutney tends to lose its green color because of the heat while processing. Using ice cubes prevents this discoloration.

**VARIATION TIP:** You can also prepare this chutney with just cilantro or mint. In fact, you can add any other greens, such as spinach or beet leaves.

PER SERVING (2 TABLESPOONS): Calories: 35; Total fat: 2g; Saturated fat: 0g; Sodium: 153mg; Carbohydrates: 4g; Sugar: 1g; Fiber: 1g; Protein: 2g

# Meetha Chutney
## (Sweet Date and Tamarind Chutney)

**PREP TIME:** 5 minutes • **COOK TIME:** 20 minutes • **MAKES ABOUT 3 CUPS**

*Meetha* means "sweet," and meetha chutney is another popular condiment in Indian cuisine alongside green chutney. This chutney is sweet and tangy and is often served with snacks and appetizers and used in chaat recipes.

---

3½ ounces seedless tamarind

¼ cup pitted dates

2½ tablespoons jaggery powder, brown sugar, or cane sugar

½ teaspoon chili powder

½ teaspoon ground cumin

¼ teaspoon salt

¼ teaspoon black salt

---

1. In a thick-bottomed pan, combine the tamarind, dates, jaggery powder, and 5 cups of water. Bring to a boil over medium heat, then reduce the heat to a simmer and cook for 15 minutes.

2. Add the chili powder, cumin, salt and black salt. Cook for another 2 minutes or until the mixture turns soft and pulpy.

3. Take the pan off the heat and allow the mixture to cool completely.

4. In a food processor or mixer grinder, process the mixture to a smooth puree, adding water if needed to achieve a thick, flowing, creamy sauce.

5. Strain the puree and transfer to an airtight container. This chutney stays for up to 5 days in the refrigerator. You can also freeze it.

**INGREDIENT TIP:** Instead of whole tamarind, you can use tamarind puree or paste.

**PREP TIP:** Instead of cooking all the ingredients in a pan, you can also pressure cook them.

PER SERVING (2 TABLESPOONS): Calories: 18; Total fat: 0g; Saturated fat: 0g; Sodium: 27mg; Carbohydrates: 5g; Sugar: 3g; Fiber: 0g; Protein: 0g

# Thakkali Thokku (Spicy Tomato Pickle)

**PREP TIME:** 5 minutes • **COOK TIME:** 35 minutes • **MAKES ABOUT 2 CUPS**

This South Indian special pickle is prepared with slow-cooked tomatoes. If you don't have any sesame oil, just use any vegetable oil. Serve as a dip, sauce, pasta sauce, or chutney over Thayir Sadam (page 82) or with chapati.

12 ripe tomatoes, coarsely chopped

10 garlic cloves, coarsely chopped

1½ teaspoons fenugreek seeds

1 teaspoon asafetida

¼ cup sesame oil

2 teaspoons mustard seeds

15 curry leaves

1½ teaspoons chili powder

1 teaspoon sea salt

1. In a food processor or mixer grinder, process the tomatoes and garlic to a puree. It doesn't have to be smooth. Set aside.

2. In a pan, dry-roast the fenugreek seeds over medium heat for 1 to 2 minutes or until they turn a shade darker.

3. Transfer the roasted seeds to a mortar and use a pestle to crush them finely while mixing in the asafetida. Set aside.

4. In the same pan, heat the sesame oil and temper the mustard seeds. When they crackle, add the curry leaves and fry for 15 seconds, then stir in the tomato puree.

5. Cook over medium heat for 30 minutes, stirring occasionally.

6. When the mixture thickens, add the chili powder, sea salt, and fenugreek seeds with asafetida.

7. Mix well and cook for another 2 minutes. The sauce should be thick and creamy.

8. Take the pan off the heat and let cool, then transfer it to an airtight container and refrigerate for up to 1 month. You can also freeze it.

**PER SERVING (2 TABLESPOONS):** Calories: 52; Total fat: 4g; Saturated fat: 1g; Sodium: 158mg; Carbohydrates: 5g; Sugar: 2g; Fiber: 2g; Protein: 1g

# Garam Masala (Indian Spice Mix)

**PREP TIME:** 5 minutes • **COOK TIME:** 45 minutes • **MAKES ABOUT 1 CUP**

Garam masala is an authentic Indian spice mix that's made using a variety of roasted and ground spices. All these spices together give garam masala a strong flavor with a slightly warming, sweet pungency. Because of its strength, use it sparingly. This aromatic spice blend is usually added toward the end of the cooking process as a way of finishing the recipe.

¼ cup cumin seeds

2 tablespoons cardamom seeds

2 tablespoons plus 1 teaspoon coriander seeds

2 tablespoons plus 1 teaspoon black peppercorns

5 cinnamon sticks

2½ teaspoons cloves

5 bay leaves

2 whole nutmegs, broken (optional)

1. In a skillet, dry-roast the cumin seeds, cardamom seeds, coriander seeds, peppercorns, cinnamon, cloves, bay leaves, and nutmeg over medium heat one at a time, each for about 2 minutes. Keep stirring until the spice turns a slightly darker shade and releases its aroma. Transfer each roasted spice to a plate. Allow to cool.

2. Once all the spices have cooled, transfer them to a food processor or mixer grinder and process to a fine powder.

3. Store the masala in an airtight container for up to 5 months.

PREP TIP: Roasting the spices helps release their flavors, but be careful to not burn them.

PER SERVING (1 TEASPOON): Calories: 6; Total fat: 0g; Saturated fat: 0g; Sodium: 1mg; Carbohydrates: 1g; Sugar: 0g; Fiber: 0g; Protein: 0g

# Vegan Ghee

**PREP TIME:** 5 minutes • **COOK TIME:** 1 hour • **MAKES 1 CUP**

*Ghee* is the Indian word for clarified butter and is one of the most important ingredients in Indian cuisine. Its rich and delicious flavor elevates any dish. Because of its high smoke point, ghee is considered one of the best cooking oils. Finally, there is a way to make ghee vegan. This recipe is inspired by South Indian street food vendors. They add tender guava leaves to sesame oil to get the same flavor as ghee made with milk. This vegan ghee has no cholesterol and comes pretty close to regular ghee.

---

1 cup organic unrefined
  virgin coconut oil

⅛ teaspoon asafetida

⅛ teaspoon ground
  turmeric

⅛ teaspoon salt

5 curry leaves

5 guava leaves

---

1.  In a pan, bring the coconut oil to a boil over medium heat.

2.  Add the asafetida, turmeric, and salt and mix well.

3.  Tear the curry leaves and guava leaves and add to the pan. Mix well and lower the heat to very low.

4.  Cook for 1 hour, stirring occasionally.

5.  Strain and transfer the ghee to a clean, dry jar. Let it cool down and then refrigerate overnight.

6.  Use this ghee in any savory recipe or any recipe that calls for ghee. Store at room temperature or in the refrigerator for up to 1 week.

**INGREDIENT TIP:** Guava leaves bring out the ghee flavor. Try to find them, but if you can't, use holy basil instead.

**VARIATION TIP:** To make vegan ghee for dessert recipes, just use coconut oil, guava leaves, and cardamom. Omit the other ingredients.

**PER SERVING (1 TEASPOON):** Calories: 39; Total fat: 4g; Saturated fat: 4g; Sodium: 6mg; Carbohydrates: 0g; Sugar: 0g; Fiber: 0g; Protein: 0g

# Soft Chapati (Wheat Flour Flatbread)

**PREP TIME:** 10 minutes • **COOK TIME:** 15 minutes • **MAKES 10 CHAPATIS**

Chapati is an integral part of the everyday Indian diet. Chapatis are rich in fiber and contain a high amount of protein and healthy fats. They're often served as a side for curries and dal. Chapati dough can be made ahead and frozen until needed.

| | | |
|---|---|---|
| 2 cups whole wheat flour, plus more for dusting | 1 teaspoon salt<br>1 tablespoon ginger paste (optional) | 2 tablespoons vegetable oil, plus more for brushing |

1. Sift the flour into a large bowl.

2. Add the salt, ginger paste (if using), and oil. Knead into a soft dough by gradually adding ¾ cup of warm water.

3. Cover the bowl with a damp cloth or plastic wrap and let it rest for 15 minutes.

4. Divide the dough into 10 golf ball–size balls.

5. To make the chapatis, heat a tawa over medium heat.

6. Keep some dry flour in a bowl on the side. Coat each ball with flour and then use a lightly floured rolling pin to roll them as thinly as possible. Dust off any excess flour.

7. Cook the chapatis one by one on the hot tawa. Keep pressing the chapati with a spatula to ensure it cooks evenly. Cook each side until you see brown spots all over.

8. Once cooked, brush both sides with oil and store in a casserole. Chapatis taste best when served hot or warm.

**INGREDIENT TIP:** Although the ginger paste is optional, it helps avoid any digestive upset caused by gluten.

PER SERVING (1 CHAPATI): Calories: 106; Total fat: 3g; Saturated fat: 0g; Sodium: 233mg; Carbohydrates: 17g; Sugar: 0g; Fiber: 3g; Protein: 3g

# No-Knead Liquid Dough Paratha

**PREP TIME:** 5 minutes • **COOK TIME:** 15 minutes • **MAKES 8 PARATHA**

This is a quick and easy no-knead version of paratha. It's mess-free, delicious, soft, and very filling. You can prepare the batter in advance and store it in the refrigerator so you can make fresh flatbreads when needed. The first paratha you cook each time usually doesn't turn out too well, but don't be discouraged; it's a bit like making pancakes. Just keep going and they'll be great. Serve with any curry or dal.

| | | |
|---|---|---|
| 1 cup all-purpose flour<br>1 teaspoon salt | 2 tablespoons<br>vegan butter<br>½ cup chopped fresh<br>cilantro | Vegetable oil,<br>for cooking |

1. In a bowl, combine the flour, salt, butter, and cilantro. Gradually add 1 cup of water to make a smooth, thick, flowing batter, like pancake batter.

2. Heat a skillet or tawa over medium heat. Pour a ladle full of batter on the tawa. Let it spread like a thick pancake.

3. Drizzle some oil around it, cover the skillet, and cook both sides evenly until it no longer sticks to the skillet and flips easily. Don't be in a hurry. It will brown a bit.

VARIATION TIP: Add some greens to increase the nutritional content of the parathas. Top the parathas with grated vegan cheese. Instead of all-purpose flour, you can use whole wheat flour. Add some minced garlic to the batter for extra flavor. You can also add thecha butter to the batter instead of plain butter.

PER SERVING (1 PARATHA): Calories: 78; Total fat: 2g; Saturated fat: 0g; Sodium: 291mg; Carbohydrates: 12g; Sugar: 0g; Fiber: 0g; Protein: 2g

# Multigrain Mixed Greens Paratha

**PREP TIME:** 10 minutes • **COOK TIME:** 20 minutes • **MAKES 12 PARATHAS**

This healthy paratha is a great way to sneak in greens and can be enjoyed for breakfast, as a snack, or as part of a larger meal.

1 cup whole wheat flour, plus more for dusting

½ cup chickpea flour (besan)

5 tablespoons jowar flour

3 tablespoons rice flour

2 tablespoons all-purpose flour

1 cup chopped mixed greens (such as spinach, cilantro, kale, beet greens)

2 teaspoons chili powder

1½ teaspoons salt

1 teaspoon garam masala

1 teaspoon ground cumin

½ teaspoon ground turmeric

1 tablespoon ginger paste

1 tablespoon garlic paste

½ cup chopped onion

¼ cup whisked plain unsweetened almond milk yogurt

Vegetable oil, for brushing

1. In a bowl, combine the wheat, chickpea, jowar, rice, and all-purpose flours. Add the mixed greens, then the chili powder, salt, garam masala, cumin, turmeric, ginger paste, garlic paste, onion, and yogurt.

2. Mix everything well together. Gradually add ½ cup of water to form a soft dough.

3. Cover the bowl with a damp cloth or plastic wrap and let it rest for 15 minutes.

4. Divide the dough into 12 golf ball–size balls. Heat a tawa over medium heat.

5. Keep some dry wheat flour in a bowl on the side. Coat each ball with flour and then use a lightly floured rolling pin to roll them as thinly as possible.

6. Cook the parathas one by one on the hot tawa. Keep pressing the paratha with a spatula to ensure it cooks evenly. Cook each side until you see brown spots all over.

7. Once cooked, brush both sides with oil and store in a casserole. Parathas taste best when served hot or warm.

PER SERVING (1 PARATHA): Calories: 99; Total fat: 2g; Saturated fat: 0g; Sodium: 313mg; Carbohydrates: 18g; Sugar: 1g; Fiber: 2g; Protein: 3g

# Spinach Garlic Naan

**PREP TIME:** 15 minutes, plus 15 minutes to rest • **COOK TIME:** 20 minutes

**MAKES 6 NAAN**

Naan is another popular flatbread that's served in Indian restaurants. It pairs well with any curry or dal and is extremely filling. Naan can be plain or flavored. There are many types of naan, such as cheese, chili, or butter, but this vegan recipe is all about spinach and garlic. Of course, if you don't like spinach or want a change, just leave it out; the naan will still be delicious.

---

5 ounces spinach

1 cup all-purpose flour

½ cup whole wheat flour, plus more for dusting

2 teaspoons kasuri methi (optional)

½ teaspoon ajwain (optional)

1 teaspoon salt

½ teaspoon baking soda

½ teaspoon powdered sugar

¼ cup whisked plain unsweetened almond milk yogurt

1 tablespoon vegetable oil

¼ cup vegan butter

6 garlic cloves, minced

2 tablespoons chopped fresh cilantro

2 green chile peppers, minced

Flavored butter, for brushing

---

1. Fill a medium pot with water and bring to a boil. Fill a bowl with ice cubes and cold water.

2. Add the spinach to the boiling water and let it blanch for 2 minutes. Using tongs or a slotted spoon, transfer the spinach to the ice bath and let it sit for 2 minutes.

3. Transfer the spinach to a food processor or mixer grinder and process to a smooth puree. Add 1 tablespoon of water if needed.

4. Sift the flours into a large bowl. Add the spinach puree, kasuri methi (if using), ajwain (if using), salt, baking soda, powdered sugar, and whisked yogurt. Mix it all together well.

5. Add the oil and 2 tablespoons of water and knead into a smooth dough.

6. Cover the bowl with plastic wrap or a damp towel and let it rest for 15 minutes.

7. Meanwhile, in a separate bowl, mix together the butter, garlic, cilantro, and green chile peppers. Set aside.

8. Divide the dough into 6 balls. Heat a tawa or griddle.

9. Coat each ball with flour and then use a lightly floured rolling pin to roll into ovals or triangles ¼ inch thick. Dust off any excess flour.

10. Brush one side of the naan with water and place the wet side on the tawa. Cook over medium heat until bubbles begin to appear. Flip and cook the other side.

11. When cooked, brush one side with flavored butter and store in a casserole.

INGREDIENT TIP: Instead of mixing two flours, you can also make this naan with just one of the flours.

PREP TIP: You can cook the naan in a tandoor if you have one.

PER SERVING (1 NAAN): Calories: 168; Total fat: 5g; Saturated fat: 1g; Sodium: 521mg; Carbohydrates: 27g; Sugar: 2g; Fiber: 2g; Protein: 5g

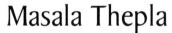

# Masala Thepla

**PREP TIME:** 10 minutes, plus 30 minutes to rest • **COOK TIME:** 20 minutes
**MAKES 8 THEPLAS**

Thepla is a popular thin, round, nutritious flatbread recipe from Gujarati cuisine. It's a thin, round flatbread that is nutritious and oh so good. There are many varieties of theplas, but this is one of my favorites.

1 cup whole wheat flour, plus more for coating

½ cup chickpea flour (besan)

1½ teaspoons salt

1 teaspoon chili powder

1 teaspoon garam masala

1 teaspoon ground coriander

1 teaspoon amchur powder

1 teaspoon cumin seeds

½ teaspoon ground turmeric

¼ cup chopped fresh cilantro

2 green chile peppers, minced

1 tablespoon ginger paste

1 tablespoon garlic paste

1 tablespoon vegetable oil, plus more for brushing

1. Sift the wheat and chickpea into a large bowl. Add the salt, chili powder, garam masala, coriander, amchur, cumin, turmeric, cilantro, green chile peppers, ginger paste, garlic paste, and oil. Mix it all well.

2. Gradually add ½ cup of water and knead into a soft dough. Brush oil all over the dough. Cover the bowl with plastic wrap or a damp cloth. Let rest for 30 minutes.

3. Divide the dough into 8 balls. Heat a tawa on medium heat.

4. Keep some dry wheat flour in a bowl on the side. Coat each ball with flour and then use a rolling pin to roll them ¼ inch thick. Dust off any excess flour.

5. Cook the theplas one by one on the hot tawa. Keep pressing the thepla with a spatula to ensure it cooks evenly. Cook each side until you see brown spots.

6. Once cooked, brush both sides with oil and store in a casserole. Theplas taste best when served hot or warm.

PER SERVING (1 THEPLA): Calories: 114; Total fat: 4g; Saturated fat: 1g; Sodium: 461mg; Carbohydrates: 16g; Sugar: 1g; Fiber: 3g; Protein: 4g

# Jowar Dill Bhakri

**PREP TIME:** 10 minutes, plus 15 minutes to rest • **COOK TIME:** 20 minutes

**MAKES 8 BHAKHRI**

Bhakhri is a Maharashtrian flatbread that's prepared with jowar (millet flour) or pearl millet (bajra). These millets are naturally gluten-free. Because the dough has no gluten, shaping the flatbreads is a different process. In this recipe, the bhakri is flavored with dill, but plain bhakri is also really good. Serve with Maharashtrian Zunka (page 112) and Golyachi Amti (page 48).

---

2 cups jowar flour or
  pearl millet

¼ cup fresh dill

6 garlic cloves, minced

2 green chile
  peppers, minced

1 teaspoon salt

---

1. Combine the jowar flour and dill in a bowl. Add the garlic, green chile peppers, and salt. Gradually add ¾ cup of warm water and knead into a soft dough.

2. Cover the bowl with a damp cloth and let it rest for 15 minutes. Heat a skillet or tawa over medium heat.

3. Divide the dough into 8 balls. Slit open a resealable plastic bag, place the dough on one side and cover with the other side. Flatten the ball as much as you can using your fingers.

4. Transfer the flattened bhakri to the hot tawa. Sprinkle water on it as it cooks. There is no need to brush it with oil. Cook both sides evenly.

**PREP TIP:** Preparing bhakri requires a little practice because it's not made the traditional way. Start with small balls and make small bhakri until you get used to the technique.

PER SERVING (1 BHAKHRI): Calories: 197; Total fat: 2g; Saturated fat: 0g; Sodium: 295mg; Carbohydrates: 38g; Sugar: 1g; Fiber: 5g; Protein: 6g

# TVP-Stuffed Flatbread

**PREP TIME:** 10 minutes, plus 20 minutes to rest • **COOK TIME:** 40 minutes
**MAKES 8 PARATHAS**

Stuffed flatbread or paratha is an extremely popular dish from the north of India. It's also served at street food stalls called dhabbas. The recipe is always divided into two parts: preparing the dough and preparing the stuffing. There are many varieties, including Kheema paratha made with minced meat. Replacing meat with TVP or soya granules makes the flatbread vegan without compromising on the taste. You can make the kheema masala and the dough separately and keep until you're ready to cook. Serve with any pickle, curry, or dal.

**FOR THE STUFFING**

1 cup TVP granules

1 tablespoon
  vegan butter

1 teaspoon cumin seeds

1 tablespoon
  ginger paste

1 tablespoon
  garlic paste

2 green chile
  peppers, minced

1 cup chopped onion

1 tablespoon kasuri
  methi (optional)

1 teaspoon chili powder

1 teaspoon ground
  coriander

1 teaspoon
  ground cumin

1 teaspoon
  garam masala

1 teaspoon
  amchur powder

1 teaspoon salt

½ teaspoon ground
  turmeric

¼ cup chopped fresh
  cilantro

**FOR THE DOUGH**

2 cups whole wheat
  flour, plus more
  for dusting

1½ teaspoons salt

1 teaspoon ajwain
  (optional)

1 tablespoon chopped
  fresh cilantro

1 tablespoon
  ginger paste

1 teaspoon vegetable oil

Vegan butter or ghee,
  for brushing

**TO MAKE THE STUFFING**

1. Cook the TVP granules as per the package instructions. Squeeze out any excess water once cooked. Set aside.

2. Heat the butter in a medium kadhai over medium heat. When it melts, fry the cumin seeds. When they crackle, add the ginger paste, garlic paste, green chile peppers, and onion. Sauté until the onion turns translucent.

3. Add the kasuri methi (if using), chili powder, coriander, ground cumin, garam masala, amchur, salt, turmeric, and 2 tablespoons of water. Mix and sauté for 30 seconds.

4. Add the cooked soya granules and cook for another 3 minutes.

5. Stir in the cilantro and take the kadhai off the heat. Allow the stuffing to cool.

**TO MAKE THE DOUGH**

6. In a large bowl, combine the whole wheat flour, salt, and ajwain (if using). Add the cilantro and ginger paste.

7. Gradually add ¾ cup of water and knead into a soft dough. Add the oil and knead again.

8. Cover the bowl with a damp cloth and let it rest for 20 minutes.

9. Divide the dough into 8 balls. Heat a tawa or a griddle.

10. Keep some dry flour in a bowl on the side. Coat each ball with flour and then use a lightly floured rolling pin to flatten them.

11. Create a depression in each and stuff with the prepared stuffing mixture. Close the dough over the stuffing and coat the ball again in flour. Flatten it carefully using a lightly floured rolling pin. Dust off any excess flour.

12. Place the paratha on the hot tawa. Cook over medium heat until brown spots begin to appear.

13. Flip and cook the other side. When cooked, brush it with butter or ghee and store in a casserole.

INGREDIENT TIP: Instead of TVP granules, you can use minced mushrooms, cauliflower, or any other veggies.

PER SERVING (1 PARATHA): Calories: 187; Total fat: 3g; Saturated fat: 0g; Sodium: 740mg; Carbohydrates: 31g; Sugar: 2g; Fiber: 7g; Protein: 12g

# Measurement Conversions

| VOLUME EQUIVALENTS | U.S. STANDARD | U.S. STANDARD (OUNCES) | METRIC (APPROXIMATE) |
|---|---|---|---|
| **LIQUID** | 2 tablespoons | 1 fl. oz. | 30 mL |
| | ¼ cup | 2 fl. oz. | 60 mL |
| | ½ cup | 4 fl. oz. | 120 mL |
| | 1 cup | 8 fl. oz. | 240 mL |
| | 1½ cups | 12 fl. oz. | 355 mL |
| | 2 cups or 1 pint | 16 fl. oz. | 475 mL |
| | 4 cups or 1 quart | 32 fl. oz. | 1 L |
| | 1 gallon | 128 fl. oz. | 4 L |
| **DRY** | ⅛ teaspoon | – | 0.5 mL |
| | ¼ teaspoon | – | 1 mL |
| | ½ teaspoon | – | 2 mL |
| | ¾ teaspoon | – | 4 mL |
| | 1 teaspoon | – | 5 mL |
| | 1 tablespoon | – | 15 mL |
| | ¼ cup | – | 59 mL |
| | ⅓ cup | – | 79 mL |
| | ½ cup | – | 118 mL |
| | ⅔ cup | – | 156 mL |
| | ¾ cup | – | 177 mL |
| | 1 cup | – | 235 mL |
| | 2 cups or 1 pint | – | 475 mL |
| | 3 cups | – | 700 mL |
| | 4 cups or 1 quart | – | 1 L |
| | ½ gallon | – | 2 L |
| | 1 gallon | – | 4 L |

## OVEN TEMPERATURES

| FAHRENHEIT | CELSIUS (APPROXIMATE) |
|---|---|
| 250°F | 120°C |
| 300°F | 150°C |
| 325°F | 165°C |
| 350°F | 180°C |
| 375°F | 190°C |
| 400°F | 200°C |
| 425°F | 220°C |
| 450°F | 230°C |

## WEIGHT EQUIVALENTS

| U.S. STANDARD | METRIC (APPROXIMATE) |
|---|---|
| ½ ounce | 15 g |
| 1 ounce | 30 g |
| 2 ounces | 60 g |
| 4 ounces | 115 g |
| 8 ounces | 225 g |
| 12 ounces | 340 g |
| 16 ounces or 1 pound | 455 g |

# Resources

**Spices and Ingredients**

    **iHerb.com:** an online grocery store

    **IndianEats.com:** an online Indian grocery store

    **Patel Brothers** (PatelBros.com): an Indian grocery store that offers a large selection of Indian spices and ingredients

    **Sprouts Market** (Sprouts.com): an online farmers' market

# Index

# Acknowledgments

I would like to thank my Amma and Appa for manifesting this dream for me. I miss you in every breath I take.

To my soul mate Kartik. My helper in shaping this book, he has assumed many roles: proofreader, recipe tester, and motivational speaker whenever I needed that extra nudge.

I would like to thank my brother Pravin for always being there for me and supporting me in all my endeavors.

To my mother-in-law, father-in-law, and sisters-in-law Vidya and Srinidhi, and my Chithi, for their constant encouragement.

To my girl gang for being my cheerleaders.

To my nieces Prashanti and Krishika. I promise to make them every recipe in this book someday.

To my fur baby, Joey. Most recipes in this book have his stamp of approval.

To Callisto Media and my editor Anne for giving me the opportunity to write my first cookbook. You fulfilled my childhood dream.

To my extended family, friends, and readers of *Cookilicious* for always believing in, supporting, and encouraging me.

# About the Author

**Priya Lakshminarayan** hails from Mumbai, India. She resides in Orlando, Florida, with her husband, Kartik, and their dog, Joey.

Priya is the creator of the award-winning vegetarian and vegan food blog *Cookilicious*. Her recipes have been featured on Buzzfeed, the Feed Feed, Smart Indian Women, Honest Cooking, and *Redbook*.

She enjoys creating recipes from scratch using fresh ingredients while listening to Bollywood music and watching *Friends* or horror movies.

She is also a proud Potterhead, globe-trotter, avid DIY-er, adrenaline junkie, board game enthusiast, and obsessive cuddler of Joey.

Visit Priya at Cookilicious.com.